Annual Survey 2010

US Government & Politics

Anthony J. Bennett

Philip Allan Updates, an imprint of Hodder Education, part of Hachette UK, Market Place, Deddington, Oxfordshire OX15 0SE

Orders
Bookpoint Ltd, 130 Milton Park, Abingdon, Oxfordshire OX14 4SB
tel: 01235 827720
fax: 01235 400454
e-mail: uk.orders@bookpoint.co.uk

Lines are open 9.00 a.m.–5.00 p.m., Monday to Saturday, with a 24-hour message answering service. You can also order through the Philip Allan Updates website: www.philipallan.co.uk

© Philip Allan Updates 2010

ISBN 978-1-4441-1042-5

First published 2010
Impression number   5   4   3   2   1
Year   2014   2013   2012   2011   2010

Printed by MPG Books, Bodmin

Hachette UK's policy is to use papers that are natural, renewable and recyclable products and made from wood grown in sustainable forests. The logging and manufacturing processes are expected to conform to the environmental regulations of the country of origin.

P01663

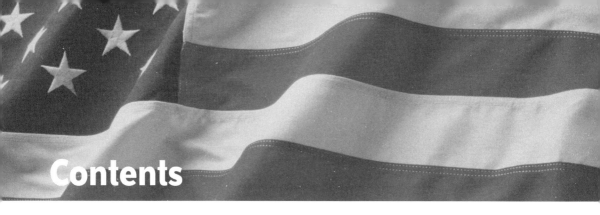

Contents

Chapter 1

George W. Bush: a failed presidency?

'A pleasant man, without any qualifications for the office.' Assessing presidents is tricky. Is this quotation a fair assessment of the 43rd president of the United States, George W. Bush? Some would say 'yes', but others would disagree. The trouble is, this comment was not made about the 43rd president, but the 32nd — none other than Franklin D. Roosevelt, probably the most highly regarded president of the twentieth century. It shows that a president's legacy is not always clear upon their leaving office. Perhaps no twentieth-century president was more highly revered upon his departure than John F. Kennedy. But here's historian Diane Kunz writing over 30 years after Kennedy's assassination:

> Fairy stories are necessary for children. Historians ought to know better. In fact, John F. Kennedy was a mediocre president. Had he obtained a second term, federal civil rights policy during the 1960s would have been substantially less productive, and US actions in Vietnam no different from what actually occurred. His tragic assassination was not a tragedy for the course of American history.

So all we can do, only a year after George W. Bush left office, is to try to offer some informed analysis of his presidency, as a first assessment rather than the final word. How history will judge him is up to historians writing a good many years — even decades — from now.

Having offered this intellectual health warning, what follows is an assessment of Bush's major achievements and failures.

Bush's achievements

There are six achievements listed here for analysis.

He served two full, consecutive terms

George W. Bush became president on 20 January 2001 and left office on 20 January 2009, serving two full and consecutive 4-year terms. This may in itself not appear much of an achievement, but it is when put in historical perspective — albeit an achievement that often goes unremarked. In the 132 years between 1877 — the accession of Rutherford Hayes — and 2009, there were 24 presidents of the United States. Only 6 of those 24 served two full and consecutive terms. Grover Cleveland managed two full terms, but they weren't consecutive. Both Teddy Roosevelt and Harry Truman managed two consecutive terms, but their first terms were slightly shorter because they took

over from presidents who had died a few months into their term of office. The only six who achieved two full and consecutive terms were Democrats Woodrow Wilson, Franklin D. Roosevelt and Bill Clinton, and Republicans Dwight Eisenhower, Ronald Reagan and George W. Bush. During the same period there were 11 one-term presidents — like Gerald Ford, Jimmy Carter and George H. W. Bush. So, even getting re-elected was an achievement.

He kept the country safe after 9/11

George W. Bush came to the presidency promising a 'humble foreign policy'. Indeed, in his 2000 election campaign he talked very little about foreign and defence policy. But then neither did his Democrat opponent that year, Al Gore. America was at peace, the Cold War was over, and there seemed few if any dark clouds on the international horizon. Here's how noted political commentator Haynes Johnson wrote about America's position at the opening of the twenty-first century in his book *The Best of Times*, published just days before 9/11:

> Americans enjoyed unprecedented peace and prosperity. No threat of global war existed. The Cold War was over. No new enemies challenged America, certainly none remotely posing the danger of a Hitler, a Stalin, a Ho Chi Minh. The 'isms' that bedevilled Americans and the world throughout the twentieth century receded into history's pages. Solid grounds existed for Americans to think their good fortune would continue, perhaps even multiply, propelling them into a more golden period.

'No new enemies' — no Osama bin Laden? 'The "isms"…receded into history's pages' — no international terrorism? Bush's presidency was in its 234th day when the planes slammed into the World Trade Center in New York City and the Pentagon in Washington DC, and White House Chief of Staff Andrew Card whispered in the President's ear as he sat reading to a class of 7-year-olds in Sarasota, Florida: 'America is under attack'.

Addressing a joint session of Congress 9 days later, the President promised:

> We will direct every resource at our command — every means of diplomacy, every tool of intelligence, every instrument of law enforcement, every financial influence, and every necessary weapon of war — to the disruption, to the defeat of the global terror network. I will not yield, I will not rest, I will not relent in waging this struggle for freedom and security for the American people.

In that moment and with these sentences, the standard for the Bush presidency was set: to protect Americans from another attack on their homeland — another 9/11 — as well as to hit Islamist terrorists and their sponsors abroad. In its editorial 4 days before the close of the Bush presidency, the *Wall Street Journal* ('The 9/11 Presidency', 16 January 2009) had this to say:

Whatever history's ultimate judgement, Mr Bush never did yield. Nearly all the significant battles of the Bush years – the Afghanistan and Iraq wars, Guantanamo and wiretapping, upheavals in the Middle East, America's troubles with Europe – stemmed directly from his response to the attacks on the Twin Towers and the Pentagon that defined his presidency.

In the weeks and months after al Qaeda had struck the United States, killing nearly 3,000 people, it seemed almost inevitable that the terrorists would attack the US mainland again. But that did not happen — in part due to the Bush administration's vigilance. In the over 7 years of Bush's presidency that followed, US law enforcement and intelligence agencies foiled numerous terrorist attempts within the United States: plots to blow up skyscrapers in Chicago and Los Angeles; to bomb the military base at Fort Dix, New Jersey; to blow up the Brooklyn Bridge in New York City.

In his farewell address to the nation (15 January 2009), the President reminded Americans of those fears of further attacks. He said of his administration's continued vigilance:

> We have not tired, we have not faltered… As the years passed, most Americans were able to return to life much as it had been before 9/11. But I never did. Every morning, I received a briefing on the threats to our nation. And I vowed to do everything in my power to keep us safe.

The trouble is that Bush's achievement is that nothing happened, and those who are protected from danger often conclude that there was no danger. Politicians rarely gain much credit for preventing something from happening. The only circumstances under which this might change for George W. Bush are if there were to be an attack on the US mainland during his successor's administration.

His legislative achievements

Given that George W. Bush had his own Republican Party in control of Congress for a majority of his presidency — $4\frac{1}{2}$ of his 8 years — one would have expected his legislative achievements to be relatively substantial. (In comparison, Bill Clinton had his Democratic Party in control of Congress for only 2 of his 8 years.) But even Bush's supporters would be pushed to come up with a lengthy list. His signature achievements came early on with the No Child Left Behind (NCLB) Act and the $1.35 trillion tax cut — both in 2001. There was a further $350 billion tax cut in 2003.

Having accused his predecessor of 'playing small ball' in terms of domestic legislation, Bush was determined to be a president who went after big-picture items. He remembered that one of his father's perceived weaknesses was not having 'the vision thing'. According to John Feehery (*Politico*, 6 January 2009):

The Bush presidency had moments of great success and dizzying failure. Bush was a man with great ambition, but his administration delivered only modest results. He made no little plans. Rather, he painted vast landscapes filled with brilliant colours. But his stroke lacked precision and at times looked amateurish. Bush attempted to drag the Republican Party up the mountain of reform and made some progress early on with success on NCLB and the Medicare Modernisation Act.

In winning in Congress, Bush possessed the art of compromise — an attribute which was often not on show in other areas of his presidency. Bush had a knack for laying out what he wanted, compromising — even giving in — and then claiming victory. With the No Child Left Behind Act, he got the godfather of the liberal Democrats, the late Senator Edward Kennedy, on board by dropping his insistence on school vouchers. He managed to claim credit for the McCain–Feingold Bipartisan Campaign Reform Act of 2002, having opposed most of it during its passage through Congress. It was much the same when it came to reorganising the intelligence agencies after 9/11. Initially, Bush wanted to create an office within the Executive Office of the President to oversee homeland security, and opposed Congress's idea of setting up a new executive department. But seeing Congress's option as the only plan that was going anywhere, Bush jumped on board, fought for it, won and claimed the credit.

It was much the same when it came to the 2003 tax cut. The President proposed a tax cut of $726 billion. The Republican-controlled House passed a $550 billion tax cut followed by the Republican-controlled Senate passing a $350 billion tax cut. The President derided Congress's proposals as he barnstormed round the country, trying to whip up support for his larger tax cut proposal. But when the conference committee reported a $350 billion tax cut back to both houses — and both chambers endorsed it — suddenly Bush was claiming as a victory the plan he had only weeks before derided. 'Sometimes I get everything I want, sometimes I don't', the President told lawmakers at a private meeting after the votes. Presidential spokesman Ari Fleischer summed it up thus:

> The President is getting less than he would have liked. He recognises that. He wishes it could have been more. But he is pleased, nevertheless, that a compromise has been reached.

If only he had adopted the same strategy when it came to immigration and social security reform in his second term.

Regime change

'Thanks to Mr Bush, more than 55 million people today, in Afghanistan and Iraq, are freed from brutal dictatorships — the Taliban in Afghanistan and Saddam Hussein's regime in Iraq', said the *Wall Street Journal*'s editorial the day before the President left office. The iconic photograph of the toppling of the statue of Saddam Hussein in Baghdad will be one of the abiding memories of the Bush presidency. Of course, I am not suggesting that the military operations in Afghanistan and Iraq were unvarnished successes, and we shall return to this matter later when we consider Bush's failures.

George W. Bush's legacy in these two states is still to be decided. Will Iraq become a stable, pro-western democracy amidst the Arab world, or will it stagger from one crisis to another, beset by sectarian violence? Certainly Bush may stand a better chance of being judged kindly on Iraq following his courageous decision to send an additional 30,000 troops there in his final 2 years, against intense partisan opposition, in what became known as the Surge.

Supreme Court appointments

Bush's most enduring achievements — at least in the eyes of conservatives — may well turn out to be his appointments of John Roberts and Samuel Alito to the US Supreme Court. Their relative youthfulness and life-time tenure mean that both these Bush appointees could still be on the Court in 20, maybe even 30, years from now. Unlike President Ford's appointment of John Paul Stevens, and Bush's father's appointment of David Souter, Roberts and Alito are unlikely to disappoint the president who nominated them. Ford and Bush Senior thought they were appointing solid conservative judges in Stevens and Souter respectively, but both appointees ended up on the liberal wing of the Supreme Court. It would appear that with Roberts and Alito, what Bush saw is what he got.

Although John Roberts was appointed as Chief Justice — with its attendant importance — it will probably be the appointment of Samuel Alito which will turn out to be Bush's biggest success. In replacing William Rehnquist with John Roberts, Bush merely replaced one conservative judge with another. However, in replacing Sandra Day O'Connor with Samuel Alito, there is much evidence already to suggest that he replaced a moderate, 'swing' justice with a conservative one. Alito's appointment has potentially swung the Court to the right, much to the pleasure of Bush's supporters.

He restored dignity to the Oval Office

American voters often look for in the president what they found missing in his predecessor. If in 1960 Dwight Eisenhower seemed a bit old and running out of steam, then how about the young, photogenic Boy Wonder — John Fitzgerald Kennedy? Looking in 1976 for someone to wipe the slate clean after all the lies of Watergate and Vietnam, then how about the clean-living, truth-telling Sunday school teacher from Georgia — Jimmy Carter?

When Governor George W. Bush pledged during his 2000 campaign to 'restore dignity to the Oval Office', everyone knew exactly what he meant. He didn't have to hold up the famous picture of the finger-wagging, red-faced President Clinton at the White House podium saying, 'I did not have sexual relations with that woman — Ms Lewinsky.' When newsreel film was broadcast in American cinemas in the late 1990s, showing President Clinton comforting female disaster victims with a perfectly innocent and proper presidential embrace, audiences sniggered. There was never any danger of them doing so when his successor was frequently filmed in an identical pose following 9/11.

Bush's failures

That George W. Bush's presidency was beset by numerous failures is clearly seen in the evidence presented in Figure 1.1 — the President's job approval rating. The graph shows its precipitate decline, especially during Bush's second term. Having reached 90% approval immediately after 9/11, the President's approval remained above 60% right through to the end of 2002, though on a downward trajectory. Bush's ratings received two boosts in 2003 — one after the fall of Baghdad in the spring, and another after the capture of Saddam Hussein at the year's end. It hovered either side of 50% in his re-election year (2004) before beginning a slow but steady decline throughout his second term, reaching into the 20% range during his last year before a final slight recovery. We shall consider six failures which partly account for this decline in public esteem.

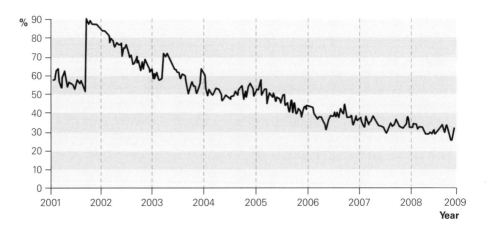

Figure 1.1 George W. Bush's job approval ratings trend (2001–09)

Source: www.gallup.com

Foreign policy failures

Where to start? The list of Bush's foreign policy failures is quite extensive: not finding weapons of mass destruction in Iraq; going into Iraq with inadequate manpower; expecting to be welcomed as liberators by the Iraqis; not having a post-Saddam plan for Iraq; the mistreatment and humiliation of prisoners at the Abu Ghraib prison in Baghdad; not capturing Osama bin Laden; appearing under a banner reading 'Mission Accomplished' on the aircraft carrier USS *Abraham Lincoln* in May 2003.

As the President faced his final press conference on 12 January 2009, he was still reluctant to describe many of these episodes as failures or mistakes. He was asked, 'Do you think in retrospect that you have made any mistakes? And if so, what is the single biggest mistake you have made?' The President answered:

> I have often said that history will look back and determine [the] mistakes I made. Clearly putting a 'Mission Accomplished' on an aircraft carrier was a mistake. It sent the wrong message. Obviously some of my rhetoric has been a mistake... There have been disappointments. Abu Ghraib obviously was a huge disappointment during the presidency. Not having [sic] weapons of mass destruction was a significant disappointment. I don't know if you want to call these mistakes or not, but they were – things didn't go according to plan, let's put it that way.

Civil liberty failures

Again, there's something of a list of failures associated with the George W. Bush presidency in terms of its failure to safeguard and protect civil rights and liberties — both of US citizens and citizens of those countries in which America was engaged in military action. The list would include: Guantánamo Bay; military tribunals; water-boarding; wiretapping; the Patriot Act. Critics may add the names of some of Bush's administration: Vice-President Dick Cheney and his chief of staff Lewis 'Scooter' Libby; Secretary of Defense Donald Rumsfeld; Attorney General Alberto Gonzales.

The President had his knuckles rapped more than once by the United States Supreme Court for what it regarded as failures to safeguard civil liberties. In the 2004 case of *Rasul* v *Bush* the Court, by a margin of 6–3, struck down some important parts of the administration's legal policy regarding its war on terrorism in general and the detainees at Guantánamo Bay in particular. The Court ruled that, contrary to the claims of the President, these detainees did have access to the United States federal courts to challenge their detention.

Two years later, in *Hamdan* v *Rumsfeld,* the Court declared unconstitutional the military commissions set up by Bush to try people at Guantánamo Bay. In 2008, in *Boumediene* v *Bush*, the Court ruled that the procedures set up by the Bush administration following the *Hamdan* decision were inadequate to ensure that the detainees received their day in court. Justice Anthony Kennedy for the Court's 5-member majority scolded the President:

> The laws and the Constitution are designed to survive, and remain in force, in extraordinary times. Liberty and security can be reconciled.

These failures in civil liberties caused significant problems for the way the United States was viewed abroad.

Hurricane Katrina

Bush's presidency, which had been transformed by a manmade disaster in September 2001, was transformed once more by a natural disaster in August 2005. The federal government in general, and the President in particular, failed to respond in a manner appropriate to the unfolding disaster that was Hurricane Katrina.

Hurricane Katrina made landfall in southeast Louisiana on 29 August 2005 as a Category 3 storm. It would turn out to be the costliest and one of the five deadliest storms ever to hit the United States. Nearly 2,000 people died from the storm and the flooding that resulted from the failure of the levées, which were meant to protect the low-lying areas of New Orleans. The nearly 3,000 deaths on 9/11 just 4 years earlier had rallied the nation around their president, but the deaths from Hurricane Katrina led to a firestorm of criticism about the way the President handled the response to the crisis. That's not to say that the state and local officials were blameless, but in a disaster of this magnitude, people look to the federal government and to their president as organiser- and comforter-in-chief.

Immediately after 9/11, President Bush had gone to Ground Zero in New York City and had rubbed shoulders with the rescuers and with those most intimately affected. After Katrina hit, however, the President seemed unfocused — to some, even disinterested. Correctly, the President put Homeland Security Secretary Michael Chertoff in charge of the federal government's response. Secretary Chertoff delegated the coordination of this response to the Director of the Federal Emergency Management Agency (FEMA), Michael Brown. The President did not visit New Orleans, the centre of the rapidly-unfolding disaster. Instead, he circled the city on Air Force One, famously photographed peering out of a window, looking down on the scene of devastation below. It was not the same as seeing the President standing on top of the rubble of the World Trade Center addressing rescuers through a bull-horn. The President looked remote and unengaged. Even while American television broadcast images of the chaotic scenes in New Orleans, the President publicly praised FEMA Director Brown in that now infamous phrase: 'Brownie, you're doing a heck of a job.' Within days, Brown resigned amid widespread public criticism of his — and the President's — handling of the disaster.

President Bush made a reference to all this in his final press conference, over 3 years later. In answer to the question as to whether, in retrospect, the President felt he had made any mistakes, Bush commented:

> I've thought long and hard about Katrina — could I have done something differently, like land Air Force One either in New Orleans or Baton Rouge? The problem with that is that law enforcement would have been pulled away from the [rescue] mission.

Bush did eventually make it to a deserted New Orleans where, in an eerie emptiness, he made his sort-of acknowledgement of failure:

> It was not a normal hurricane, and the normal disaster relief system was not equal to it. When the federal government fails to meet such an obligation, I as president am responsible for the problem, and for the solution.

As Bush biographer Robert Draper (*Dead Certain*, 2007) commented: 'Blinking, one might have missed it — but there it was, the President owning up to his share of the blame.'

He alienated conservatives

It's when politicians lose the support of their own base that problems abound. One expects one's opponents to oppose. But when leading your own supporters, attacks from behind can be lethal — what Professor Anthony King once described as 'over-the-shoulder politics'. In too many ways, Bush alienated his conservative base.

There was Bush's profligate federal spending — increasing at a faster rate than under any president since Lyndon Johnson. Then there was Bush's refusal to wield the veto pen at all during his first term, even though conservatives were crying out for him to veto what they saw as wasteful spending from Congress. He waited until the 66th month of his presidency to use his first veto, and used only 11 regular vetoes and one pocket veto during his 8 years in office. Bush further alienated conservatives by signing the McCain–Feingold Bipartisan Campaign Reform Act in 2002, a piece of legislation they would have loved to have seen him veto. Then, towards the end of his presidency, there was Bush giving out $700 billion of taxpayers' money in the Wall Street and bank bailout scheme.

The one act of the Bush presidency which may have riled conservatives more than any other was the President's nomination of Harriet Miers to the United States Supreme Court. The vacancy occurred following the retirement of Justice Sandra Day O'Connor, a moderate conservative judge who nonetheless often took more liberal positions on such issues as abortion and affirmative action. Here was Bush's opportunity to swing the Court to the right by replacing O'Connor with a dyed-in-the-wool conservative. However, the President nominated a personal friend, a judicial unknown, vouching for her with the infamous remark: 'I've known Harriet for more than a decade, I know her heart, I know her character.' Conservative commentator Charles Krauthammer called on Bush to withdraw the nomination:

> There are 1,084,504 lawyers in the United States. What distinguishes Harriet Miers from any of them, other than her connection with the President? By choosing a nominee suggested by Senate Democratic leader Harry Reid and well known only to himself, the President ducked a fight on the most important domestic question dividing liberals from conservatives: the

principles by which one should read and interpret the Constitution. For a presidency marked by a courageous willingness to think and do big things, this nomination is a sorry retreat into smallness.

Under a firestorm of criticism from his own side, the President allowed Miers to withdraw from the nomination. In her place, he nominated — and the Republican-controlled Senate confirmed — a true conservative, Judge Samuel Alito, but the damage was done.

Presided over ballooning deficits and economic collapse

In almost every economic indicator, the Bush years came up short. Although the President liked to boast of the '52 months of uninterrupted economic growth' which had occurred on his watch, by the time Bush left office, most Americans agreed that economically the nation was heading in the wrong direction. And with good reason.

When George W. Bush arrived in Washington (January 2001), unemployment stood at 4.2%. In his last full month in office (December 2008), unemployment had reached 7.2%. A week before his presidency began, the Dow Jones Industrial Average stood at 11,723; by 15 September 2008, it was 7,552, having lost over 35% of its value. President Clinton bequeathed Bush a federal budget surplus of $120 billion; by 2008 the federal budget was in deficit to the tune of $420 billion. Figure 1.2 shows that the national debt rocketed during the Bush years, while Figure 1.3 shows that US house prices fell through the floor. The number of jobs in the US increased by just 2% over Bush's 8 years — the weakest growth since such data started to be collected 70 years ago. GDP grew at the slowest pace for a period of 8 years since the Truman administration. Americans' income grew more slowly than during any presidency since the 1960s, other than that of Bush Senior.

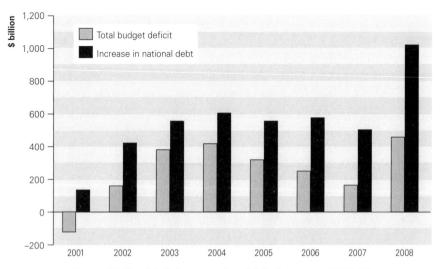

Figure 1.2 Total deficits vs. national debt increases, 2001–08

US Government & Politics

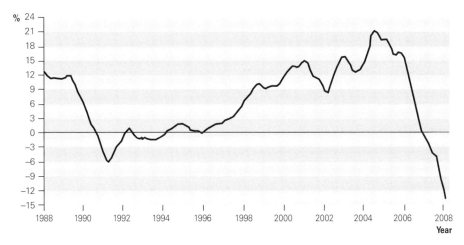

Figure 1.3 US house prices: percentage yearly change in single family homes,
top 20 metro areas, 1988–2008

Source: Standard & Poor/Case Schiller index

Personal failings

Finally, there were Bush's personal failings. In many ways, George W. Bush was a likeable person: affable; a good sense of humour; moral; a good role model; a committed Christian who practised what he preached. But what some saw as strengths, others saw as weaknesses. To his supporters, he was decisive; to his critics he was arrogant. Conservative commentator David Brooks described him as both 'outrageously self-confident' and 'stubborn'. Furthermore, traits that were a strength in one situation turned into a weakness in another. The *Washington Post*'s final editorial on Bush (18 January 2009) remarked:

> His certitude amid the crisis of September 11 helped galvanise the initial national response, including the toppling of the Taliban in Afghanistan. Alas, that same certitude led Mr Bush down many blind alleys and, in the worst moments, caused him to debase the country's moral currency.

According to John Dickerson and Karen Tumulty in *Time* magazine:

> To some, the way Bush walks and talks and smiles is the body language of courage and self-assurance, and of someone who shares their values. But to others, it is the swagger and smirk that signals the certainty of the stubbornly simpleminded.

Bush liked to depict himself as 'the decider'. Just 7 months into his presidency — a fortnight or so before 9/11 — a pupil at an elementary school in his home town of Crawford, Texas, asked him if it was 'hard to make decisions' as president. Bush replied:

> Not really. If you know what you believe, decisions come pretty easy. If you're one of those types of people that are always trying to figure out which

way the wind is blowing, decision-making can be difficult. But I know who I am. I know what I believe in, and I know where I want to lead this country.

White House speechwriter David Frum described Bush as 'relentlessly disciplined' yet also 'sometimes glib, even dogmatic; often incurious and as a result ill-informed; more conventional in his thinking than a leader should probably be.'

Certainly George W. Bush was no Ronald Reagan — no great communicator. 'Bushisms' abounded throughout his presidency. Even in his final press conference, as he tried to wish his successor well, the President managed another example of his infamously mangled syntax:

> I'm telling you there's an enemy that would like to attack America again. There just is. That's the reality of the world. And I wish him all the very best.

The Bush legacy

Bush's political effect on the Republican Party bordered on the disastrous. Compared with 2004, the Republicans in 2008 won 9 fewer states, which between them commanded 113 Electoral College votes. Combining 2006 and 2008, they also lost 14 seats in the Senate, 54 seats in the House and 6 state governorships. After the 2006 mid-term elections, Bush admitted that 'it was a thumping' as far as the Republicans were concerned. And in 2008, the Republicans nominated as their presidential candidate someone who was the most un-Bush-like of all their potential nominees — John McCain. McCain desperately tried to distance himself from his own president. Bush did not campaign for him; McCain studiously avoided mentioning Bush in his speeches and in his television appearances; Bush did not even appear in person at the party's nominating convention — the first time in 40 years that the incumbent president was a no-show at his party's convention.

The highs and lows of the Bush presidency, in his own words...

'I can hear you. The rest of the world hears you. And the people who knocked these buildings down will hear all of us soon.'

New York City, 14 September 2001

'Either you are for us, or you are with the terrorists.'

Address to Congress, 21 September 2001

'My fellow Americans, major combat operations in Iraq have ended. In the battle of Iraq, the United States and our allies have prevailed.'

On board *USS Abraham Lincoln*, 1 May 2003

'There are some [in Iraq] who feel like that the conditions are such they can attack us there. My answer is, bring 'em on.'

July 2003

'You may not always agree with me, but you know where I stand.'
> Acceptance speech at the Republican National Convention, September 2004

'I earned political capital in this campaign, and now I intend to spend it. It's my style.'
> After 2004 election

'Brownie, you're doing a heck of a job.'
> On FEMA Director Michael Brown, September 2005

'I know her. I know her heart. I know what she believes.'
> On Harriet Miers, 4 October 2005

'I hear the voices, and I read the front page, and I know the speculation. But I'm the decider, and I decide what's best.'
> On his keeping Donald Rumsfeld as Defense Secretary, April 2006

'It was a thumping.'
> On the 2006 mid-term elections, 8 November 2006

'Hey, that's what happens when you have a free society!'
> On the shoe-throwing incident during his press conference in Baghdad, 2008

According to James Ceaser (*The Epic Journey*, 2009):

> George W. Bush was not on the ballot in 2008, but he might just as well have been. For according to [Obama strategists] David Axelrod and David Plouffe, all that was wrong with the United States could be summarised in one word: Bush.

It was the Democrats who talked about Bush, not Republicans. One can see this most clearly by analysing the number of times per 25,000 words that the President's name was mentioned at the Democratic and Republican national conventions: 46 times at the Democratic convention; a mere 7 times at the Republican convention. During the three presidential televised debates, Bush was mentioned 27 times — 21 times by Barack Obama and just 6 times by John McCain. Indeed, McCain came up with one of his best lines in the debates by disassociating himself from Bush:

> Senator Obama, I am not President Bush. If you wanted to run against President Bush, you should have run four years ago.

What immediate legacy have commentators and presidency-watchers ascribed to Bush? In an unscientific poll of 109 historians conducted in April 2008 by the History News Network, more than 60% rated Bush as 'the worst in US history'. The more respected 2009 C-SPAN presidential leadership survey posted Bush as 36th out of the 42 presidents. His nearest postwar colleague was Richard Nixon at 27th, and the only twentieth-century president below him was Warren Harding (1921–23) at 38th. That's quite damning.

Not everyone would agree, however. Jonathan Rauch, in a *National Journal* cover story ('Small Ball After All?', 20 September 2008) concluded that 'whichever view one takes, Bush was a game-changing president, a transformative figure rather than one who plays "small ball".' According to the *Washington Post* (editorial, 18 January 2009), Bush exited with 'a legacy of grave errors and mismanagement, but also of promoting just causes', perhaps none more so than in Africa, where he spent more on fighting the scourge of HIV/AIDS than any other president.

According to Bush biographer Robert Draper, 'the nation very much needed a president with [Bush's] level of certitude, with that clarity of vision such that he could say, "you're either for us or you're for the terrorists"', adding that Bush 'brought forth from the public a great amount of pride in America and a great amount of determination'.

Most commentators stress that the jury is still out on Bush, and that so much depends on what happens regarding international terrorism and in Iraq. Michael Gerson of the *Washington Post* concluded that George W. Bush 'is going to be judged on whether he was right about the conduct of the war on terror.' Professor George Edwards cautions that 'if Iraq should turn into a stable democracy and a model for the Middle East that will be a huge plus in his legacy.' Edwards, one of the most astute scholars of the presidency, concludes that 'history will view this as a consequential presidency. George W. Bush was one who thought boldly and aimed explicitly to make a lasting impact.' To discover what that lasting impact will be — and whether or not George W. Bush will ultimately be seen as a failed president — we must await the judgement of history.

Questions

1 What six achievements does the chapter attribute to George W. Bush?
2 How unusual is it for a president to serve two full, consecutive terms?
3 How did the President's speech to Congress on 20 September 2001 'set the standard' for the Bush presidency?
4 What were the major legislative achievements of the Bush presidency?
5 Why was Samuel Alito's nomination to the Supreme Court more significant than that of John Roberts?
6 Why did George W. Bush think there was a need to 'restore dignity to the Oval Office'?
7 What six failures does the chapter attribute to George W. Bush?
8 What evidence does Figure 1.1 give for Bush's presidency being a failure?
9 Analyse Bush's response at his 12 January 2009 press conference to the question: 'Do you think in retrospect you have made any mistakes?'
10 In what ways did George W. Bush fail to protect civil rights and liberties?
11 Why did Hurricane Katrina become a problem for the Bush administration?
12 How did George W. Bush alienate conservatives?

13 What do Figures 1.2 and 1.3 show about the economic problems facing the United States during the Bush years?
14 What personal failings of George W. Bush are mentioned in the chapter?
15 To what extent is Bush something of a paradox as a person?
16 What effect did the Bush presidency have on the Republican Party?
17 What effect did President Bush have on the 2008 presidential election campaign?
18 Summarise your conclusions about the success or failure of the Bush presidency. What kind of legacy do you think he will leave?

Chapter 2

The Supreme Court

What you need to know

- The Supreme Court is the highest federal court in the USA.
- Of the nine justices who served in the two terms we consider in this chapter, seven had been appointed by Republican presidents and only two by Democrats.
- The Supreme Court has the power of judicial review. This is the power to declare acts of Congress or actions of the executive branch — or acts or actions of state governments — unconstitutional, and thereby null and void.
- By this power of judicial review, the Court acts as the umpire of the Constitution and plays a leading role in safeguarding Americans' rights and liberties.

Having dedicated the whole of the 2009 *Annual Survey* to coverage of the presidential election, in this edition we consider both the 2007–08 and 2008–09 terms on the Supreme Court.

The 2007–08 term

The 2007–08 term of the Supreme Court was the third full term under Chief Justice John Roberts. The term will be remembered for handing down one notable landmark decision — on the Second Amendment — as well as other important decisions concerning the death penalty and the rights of detainees at Guantánamo Bay. Table 2.1 shows the cases from the 2007–08 term that we shall be considering in this chapter.

Conduct of elections

The Supreme Court in 2007–08 handed down two important decisions regarding the conduct of elections. In *Crawford* v *Marion County Election Board*, the Court upheld an Indiana state voter identification law which required that would-be voters produce a current state or federal photo ID to cast an election ballot. The Court rejected the view 'that the law substantially burdens the right to vote in violation of the Fourteenth Amendment; that it is neither a necessary nor appropriate method of avoiding election fraud;

Table 2.1 Significant Supreme Court decisions, 2007–08 term

Case	Concerning	Decision
Crawford v *Marion County Election Board*	Photo ID required to vote	6–3
Davis v *Federal Election Commission*	Campaign finance	5–4
District of Columbia v *Heller*	Washington DC handgun ban	5–4
Baze v *Rees*	Lethal injection	7–2
Kennedy v *Louisiana*	Death penalty for child rape	5–4
Boumediene v *Bush*	Rights of Guantánamo Bay detainees	5–4

that it will arbitrarily disenfranchise qualified voters who do not possess the required identification and will place an unjustified burden on those who cannot obtain such identification.' The Court's majority decided that the benefits of reducing voter fraud outweighed any inconvenience to voters of having to go to the local Bureau of Motor Vehicles, pose for a photograph and pick up the relevant documentation. Even the three dissenters — Justices Breyer, Ginsburg and Souter — approved of states passing laws to cut down on voter fraud, though they felt that Indiana's was unnecessarily burdensome.

In *Davis* v *Federal Election Commission*, the Court was ruling on parts of the so-called McCain–Feingold campaign finance law, passed in 2002. In this particular case, the Court was ruling on the constitutional validity of what has become known as the 'millionaire's amendment'. The 2002 law requires candidates who finance their own campaigns to disclose more information and allows their opponents to raise more money. Specifically, where candidates for the House of Representatives spend more than $350,000 of their own money, the law allows their opponents to receive triple the usual amounts from individuals — $6,900 rather than $2,300 — when a complex statutory formula is met. The case was brought by the Democrat Jack Davis, who twice ran for the House of Representatives from New York, spending or lending himself millions of dollars of his own money. He lost both elections. Davis's lawyers claimed the law had a hidden motive — that of protecting incumbents from rich challengers. Writing for the five-member majority, Justice Samuel Alito declared the provision unconstitutional because it 'imposes an unprecedented penalty on any candidate who robustly exercises' free speech rights guaranteed by the First Amendment. By this provision, claimed Justice Alito, rich candidates would have to 'choose between the First Amendment right to engage in unfettered political speech and subjection to discriminatory fundraising limitations.' He continued:

Different candidates have different strengths. Some are wealthy; others have wealthy supporters who are willing to make large contributions. Some are celebrities; others have the benefit of a well-known family name. Levelling electoral opportunities means making and implementing judgements about which strengths should be permitted to contribute to the outcome of an election. The Constitution confers upon voters, not Congress, the power to choose the members of the House of Representatives.

Alito was joined in his majority opinion by his fellow conservative justices — John Roberts, Antonin Scalia and Clarence Thomas — as well as by Anthony Kennedy.

We commented in the 2008 edition of this *Annual Survey* on the significance in some cases of the switch that took place in 2006 of Justice Samuel Alito for Justice Sandra O'Connor. We saw a number of cases in which Alito took a more conservative position than his predecessor. This factor was on view in the *Davis* v *Federal Election Commission* case too. Back in 2003, Justice O'Connor was the co-author of a decision by the Supreme Court —*McConnell* v *FEC* — in which the Court, by 5 votes to 4, substantially upheld the major provisions of the McCain–Feingold law. On that occasion, Justice O'Connor sided with the four liberal justices — Stevens, Souter, Ginsburg and Breyer — in upholding the law. In this case, O'Connor's replacement, Justice Alito, authored the majority opinion that struck down a provision of the same law, giving the conservative justices the majority which alluded them 5 years earlier.

Writing for the dissenting liberals, Justice John Paul Stevens stated that 'reducing the importance of wealth as a criterion for public office and countering the perception that seats in the United States Congress are available for purchase by the wealthiest bidder' offered valid justifications for the law's provision.

Gun laws and the Second Amendment

The case of *District of Columbia* v *Heller* was the Supreme Court's one great landmark decision of the 2007–08 term. It will be discussed for years to come, as it was the first time that the Court had offered a clear ruling on the meaning of the Second Amendment's right to 'keep and bear arms'. The case centred on a gun law introduced in Washington DC in 1976 which banned the ownership of handguns and required that shotguns and rifles be kept in the owner's home, unloaded and dismantled or bound by a trigger lock.

Writing for the Court's five-member majority, Justice Antonin Scalia stated:

> We hold that the District's ban on handgun possession in the home violates the Second Amendment, as does the prohibition against rendering any lawful firearm in the home operable for the purpose of immediate self-defence. [The Second Amendment] surely elevates above all other interests the right of law-abiding, responsible citizens to use arms in defence of hearth and home.

Scalia was joined by his fellow conservative justices — John Roberts, Clarence Thomas and Samuel Alito — as well as by 'swing' justice, Anthony Kennedy.

Writing for the Court's dissenting minority, Justice Stephen Breyer claimed that the decision 'threatens to throw into doubt the constitutionality of gun laws throughout the United States', calling the decision a 'formidable and potentially dangerous' mission for the courts to undertake. He was joined by liberal colleagues John Paul Stevens, David Souter and Ruth Bader Ginsburg.

What does the Second Amendment actually say about the right to carry guns? The wording, as well as the punctuation, is curious:

> A well regulated Militia, being necessary to the security of a free State, the right of the people to keep and bear Arms, shall not be infringed.

So what does this mean? Is it a guarantee of a right to form 'a well regulated militia' — a *collective* right to keep and bear arms — or does it guarantee an *individual* right? Liberals, Democrats and friends of the Brady Campaign to Prevent Gun Violence have taken the former view. Conservatives, Republicans and paid-up members of the National Rifle Association (NRA) have taken the latter view. With the exception of a rather obscure ruling back in 1939, in the case of *United States* v *Miller*, the Supreme Court has pretty much kept out of the debate. The decision in this 2008 case was music to the ears of the NRA and their (mainly) Republican friends, including President George W. Bush. On the day of the Court's ruling, President Bush stated:

> As a longstanding advocate of the rights of gun owners in America, I applaud the Supreme Court's historic decision today confirming what has always been clear in the Constitution: The Second Amendment protects an individual right to keep and bear firearms.

How did the justices arrive at such differing conclusions about the meaning of 27 words? First, we need to divide the Second Amendment into two clauses — what we might call the preface ('A well regulated militia, being necessary to the security of a free state') and the operative clause ('the right of the people to keep and bear arms, shall not be infringed'). Justice Scalia for the majority concludes that the preface does not limit or expand the scope of the operative clause but grants *to each individual* the right to bear arms, and this right is not a *collective* one linked to joining a militia. He draws attention to the fact that the First, Fourth and Ninth Amendments all refer to *individual* rights and not to collective rights 'exercised only through participation in some corporate body.' But Justice Stevens for the minority believes that the preface's mention of a well-regulated militia means that the right to bear arms is tied to service in a militia. He points out that the majority are restricting the meaning of the Second Amendment by limiting it to 'law abiding, responsible citizens'.

The two sides then go on to debate the meaning of the phrase 'to keep and bear arms'. Justice Scalia states that 'the most natural reading of "keep arms" is to "have weapons".' He believes that '"keep arms" was simply a common way [in the eighteenth century, when the Amendment was formulated] of referring to possessing arms, both for militiamen and everyone else.' But Justice Stevens takes a different view:

> A number of state militia laws in effect at the time of the Amendment's drafting used the term 'keep' to describe the requirement that militia members store their arms at their homes, ready to be used for service when necessary.

For Justice Stevens, the term 'bear arms' is 'a familiar idiom meaning to serve as a soldier, do military service, fight' — as defined by the Oxford English Dictionary.

What, therefore, are the likely results of this decision? First, there will have to be a new gun law for the District of Columbia that will pass muster with the Supreme Court. Second, expect more challenges to the gun laws in other jurisdictions, most notably in Chicago. Third, expect challenges to federal laws which limit gun ownership and usage. But we need to be cautious, for contained in Scalia's 64-page decision was this warning to gun enthusiasts:

> Nothing in our [majority] opinion should be taken to cast doubt on long-standing prohibitions on the possession of firearms by felons and the mentally ill, or laws forbidding the carrying of firearms in sensitive places such as schools and government buildings, or laws imposing conditions and qualifications on the commercial sale of arms.

Justice Scalia admitted that, like most other freedoms, this particular freedom is not without reasonable limitations. But as Mike Hammond, counsel for Gun Owners of America, remarked immediately after the Court's decision was announced: 'This is the beginning of litigation rather than the end. I suspect we'll spend the next 50 years fighting over what [this decision] means.'

Death penalty

In recent terms the Supreme Court has chipped away at the death penalty, declaring it unconstitutional, for example, to execute the mentally retarded or those who committed their crimes while under the age of 18. The Court ruled that to do so contravened the ban in the Eighth Amendment on 'cruel and unusual punishments'.

In this term the Court made two further important rulings regarding the meaning of the Eighth Amendment. In a 7–2 ruling in *Baze* v *Rees*, the Court upheld Kentucky's use of lethal injection as its method of execution in death penalty cases. The method authorised in Kentucky is the same as that in

34 other states as well as that used by the federal government, so a ban on lethal injection would have had significant repercussions.

Writing for the 7-member majority, Chief Justice John Roberts declared:

> Simply because an execution method may result in pain, either by accident or as an inescapable consequence of death, does not establish the sort of 'objectively intolerable risk of harm' that qualifies as cruel and unusual.

The one real surprise was the inclusion in the decision of a declaration by Justice John Paul Stevens that his 33-year tenure on the Court had led him to believe that capital punishment *per se* is unconstitutional. The two dissenters in this case, Antonin Scalia and Clarence Thomas, took an altogether different view of the matter. To them, a method of execution could constitute a cruel and unusual punishment 'only if it is deliberately designed to inflict pain'. Concluded Scalia and Thomas:

> Judged under that standard, this is an easy case: Because it is undisputed that Kentucky adopted its lethal injection protocol in an effort to make capital punishment more humane, not to add elements of terror, pain or disgrace to the death penalty, the petitioner's challenge must fail.

In another death penalty decision, the Court declared a Louisiana state law which provided for the death penalty in cases of child rape to be unconstitutional. The decision, *Kennedy* v *Louisiana*, brought another 5–4 decision, and Justice Anthony Kennedy again provided the critical fifth vote, this time siding with liberals John Paul Stevens, David Souter, Ruth Bader Ginsburg and Stephen Breyer. Indeed, the Court went further, announcing that any crime against an individual — as opposed to an offence against the state, such as treason — 'where the life of the victim was not taken' could not be punishable by the death penalty. 'We cannot sanction [the death penalty] when the harm to the victim, though grave, cannot be quantified in the same way as the death of the victim', concluded Justice Kennedy. This was the fourth limit on the death penalty announced by the Court since 2002 (*Atkins* v *Virginia*), when the Court barred the execution of the mentally retarded. In 2005 (*Roper* v *Simmons*), it barred the death penalty for crimes committed by under-18s, and in 2007 (*Panetti* v *Quarterman*) it barred the execution of schizophrenics.

For the dissenting majority, made up of the Court's four conservatives, Justice Samuel Alito claimed that the Court had no power 'to strike down federal or state criminal laws on the ground that they are not in the best interests of crime victims or the broader society.'

Rights of Guantánamo Bay detainees
For the third time in 4 years, the Supreme Court dealt a significant blow to the Bush administration's policy regarding the rights of detainees at Guantánamo

Bay. In 2004, in the case of *Rasul* v *Bush*, the Court had declared (6–3) that, contrary to the claims of the Bush White House, the foreign detainees at Guantánamo Bay did have access to the United States federal courts to challenge their detention. Then in 2006, in *Hamdan* v *Rumsfeld*, the Court declared that the military commissions set up by President Bush to try suspected members of Al Qaeda held at Guantánamo Bay were unconstitutional. However, despite these rulings, by 2008 none of the Guantánamo Bay detainees had been given access to the federal courts. Hence another case, *Boumediene* v *Bush*, brought on behalf of 37 foreigners at the Guantánamo Bay camp. All were captured on foreign soil and declared as 'enemy combatants' by the Bush administration. All have protested their innocence and had tried, unsuccessfully, to gain access to the federal courts. 'The costs of delay can no longer be borne by those who are held in custody', wrote Justice Anthony Kennedy in the majority 5–4 opinion.

The judgement in *Boumediene* included a severe rebuke for the policies of the Bush administration which had claimed that, as America is at war, the President has special powers to ensure the safety of the nation. 'The laws and Constitution are designed to survive, and remain in force, in extraordinary times', wrote Justice Kennedy for the majority, joined by the Court's liberal wing — Justices Stevens, Souter, Ginsburg and Breyer. 'To hold that the political branches may switch the Constitution on or off at will would lead to a regime in which they, not this court, could say "what the law is"', he added, using language from the famous 1803 *Marbury* v *Madison* decision.

The minority — Roberts, Scalia, Thomas and Alito — agreed with the President's position. 'America is at war with radical Islamists', wrote Justice Scalia in the dissenting opinion, adding that the decision 'will almost certainly cause more Americans to be killed.' (There might have been a certain irony in this remark when, just 2 weeks later, Scalia read the majority opinion in *District of Columbia* v *Heller*, which struck down the District's handgun ban.) 'The Nation will live to regret what the Court has done today', concluded Scalia on this occasion. President Bush was disappointed with the ruling. 'We'll abide by the Court's position', said the President, 'but that doesn't mean I have to agree with it.'

In response to previous Court decisions, Congress had passed the 2006 Military Commission Act, which removed from the federal courts their jurisdiction to hear the cases filed by Guantánamo Bay detainees challenging the grounds of their detention. It was this law that the Court declared unconstitutional in the *Boumediene* case. The decision left the Bush administration's Guantánamo Bay strategy in disarray and a significant problem in the intray of the incoming administration in January 2009. David Cole, a professor at the Georgetown University Law Centre in Washington DC, stated that the *Boumediene* decision left 'more unanswered questions than answered questions' about the shape and scope of the hearings the Supreme Court thought the detainees ought to be granted.

Court statistics: 2007–08

In the 2007–08 term, the Supreme Court delivered 67 opinions, beating by 1 the unusually low number of 68 opinions in 2006–07. This seems to confirm the presumption that Chief Justice John Roberts is continuing his predecessor's policy of cutting down on the number of cases heard by the Court each term. Of the 67 opinions delivered, only 11 (17%) were 5–4 decisions, down from the unusually high 33% in the previous term. The distribution of justices in 5–4 decisions was less predictable along ideological lines than it was in the previous term. Of the 11 instances of 5–4 decisions, 7 were decided along ideological lines, and of these 7 the conservative majority on the Court (led by Chief Justice Roberts and joined by Associate Justices Antonin Scalia, Clarence Thomas and Samuel Alito) prevailed in 4. In the previous term, Justice Anthony Kennedy was in the majority of all 24 of the 5–4 cases, but in 2007–08 was in the majority in only 7 of the 11 5–4 decisions. He was, though, the 'swing' vote in all 4 of the landmark 5–4 decisions we have considered for this term.

The justice most frequently in the majority during the 2007–08 term was Chief Justice John Roberts — the second time in the 3 years Roberts has been on the Court that he has held this distinction. He was in the majority in 60 of the 67 cases (90%), followed by Anthony Kennedy — last year's leading majority justice — with an 86% score.

The two justices most frequently in agreement were Chief Justice Roberts and Associate Justice Antonin Scalia — the first time since they joined the Court that Roberts and Alito had not held this distinction. But there was no change from the previous term in the two justices who most frequently disagreed. As in 2006–07, it was the two Republican-appointed justices John Paul Stevens and Clarence Thomas who disagreed on 55% of the term's non-unanimous cases. Thomas enjoyed the same level of disagreement with Justice Stephen Breyer.

The 2008–09 term

No truly landmark decisions were handed down in the 2008–09 term of the Supreme Court. The one case that came to public attention probably did so because of its link to the nomination of Sonia Sotomayor to the Court, rather than because it was a landmark decision. In the case of *Ricci* v *DeStefano*, the Supreme Court reversed a federal appeals court decision in which Judge Sotomayor had concurred. The case concerned the matter of race in the hiring and promotion of workers in the public sector — in other words, it was about the constitutional status of affirmative action programmes.

Background to the 2009 affirmative action case

The case revolved around the promotion of firefighters in New Haven, Connecticut. New Haven firefighters seeking promotion to the rank of lieutenant or captain had to sit a written test and attend an interview. When the test results were published, it was clear that no African Americans and only two Hispanics would have been eligible for immediate promotion. City officials then threw out the test results and denied promotion to any of the eligible candidates, saying that they feared a lawsuit on behalf of the African Americans. Frank Ricci, a white firefighter, was thereby denied promotion and took his case to the federal courts. Both the trial court and the appeals court found against him. In the latter case, all three judges — including Judge Sotomayor — stated that Ricci had not been unfairly treated. Ricci appealed his case to the US Supreme Court.

However, the facts of the case included details suggesting that the New Haven city officials had made their decision more out of political convenience than judicial concern. The tests which the firefighters had to sit were agreed to be racially non-discriminatory. Had they not been, this would have been grounds for a lawsuit by minority workers. The professional firm used by New Haven to conduct the tests and interviews based their practices on detailed research to ensure that the questions were job-related and administered in a race-neutral way. The three-person interviewing teams were all made up of one white member, one Hispanic and one African American. So why did the New Haven officials fear a lawsuit if they accepted the results of such a selection process? If one was brought, would it not anyway have been likely to fail? And regardless of that, is fear of judicial action grounds for setting aside a fair and legal selection?

More troubling were details reported by the *National Journal* in a piece by Stuart Taylor, entitled *Firefighters Case: What Really Happened* (13 June 2009). Once the results of the tests and interviews were announced, politically powerful African Americans led by Reverend Boise Kimber — a longstanding supporter of New Haven's mayor and a key vote-getter for him — demanded that no white or Hispanic firefighters be promoted. The mayor, John DeStefano, told aides that he would block all promotions, even if the city's civil service board approved the tests as fair and valid.

The Supreme Court's judgement

The Supreme Court reversed the lower courts' decisions and in a 5–4 ruling declared that Frank Ricci and his other white colleagues had faced workplace discrimination on the basis of race. Writing for the majority, Justice Anthony Kennedy — joined by the Court's four conservatives (Scalia, Thomas, Roberts and Alito) — declared:

> No individual should face workplace discrimination based on race. Fear of litigation alone cannot justify an employer's reliance on race to the detriment

of individuals who passed examinations and qualified for promotions. The process was open and fair. The problem, of course, is that after the tests were completed, the raw racial results became the predominant rationale for the city's refusal to certify the results.

The decision was clearly a victory not only for the white firefighters, but also for conservative interest groups who said that the city's decision had amounted to denying promotions on the basis of skin colour.

Writing for the minority, Justice Ruth Bader Ginsburg tried to argue that the New Haven officials and the lower federal courts had been right in their decisions because 'firefighting is a profession in which the legacy of racial discrimination casts an especially long shadow', while admitting that the white firefighters 'understandably attract the court's sympathy'. Justice Samuel Alito, in a concurring majority opinion, said that the city's decision was driven more by racial politics than any legitimate concerns about the test, rounding on Justice Ginsburg's argument by stating: 'The plaintiffs do not demand "sympathy" but even-handed enforcement of the law.'

Court statistics: 2008–09

In the 2008–09 term, the Supreme Court delivered 74 opinions — its highest number since 2004–05. Of these 74 opinions, 23 (31%) were 5–4 decisions, significantly up on the unusually low figure of the previous term (see Table 2.2). However, the distribution of justices in the 5–4 decisions was more ideologically predictable. In 16 of these 23 decisions (70%), all four members of the court's liberal wing (Stevens, Souter, Ginsburg and Breyer) were on one side and all four of the court's conservative wing (Scalia, Thomas, Roberts and Alito) were on the other. Between them was swing justice Anthony Kennedy — described by Adam Liptak in the *New York Times* as 'the most powerful judge in America' (1 July 2009). Kennedy joined the liberals five times and the conservatives 11 times, a significant shift from the previous term, in which Kennedy had divided his support much more evenly. The result was a discernable rightward shift in the Court during 2008–09. Indeed, Justice Kennedy was the deciding vote in *Ricci* v *DeStefano* which we have just considered, siding with the court's four conservatives.

Table 2.2 Supreme Court statistics, 2003–09

	2003–04	2004–05	2005–06	2006–07	2007–08	2008–09
Number of cases	73	74	69	68	67	74
Decided by 5–4 (%)	25	30	23	35	17	31
Justice most frequently in the majority	O'Connor	Breyer	Roberts	Kennedy	Roberts	Kennedy

Anthony Kennedy was the justice most frequently in the majority during the 2008–09 term, as he was in 2006–07. (He was placed second in this ranking in 2007–08.) Kennedy was in the majority in 89% of the cases, followed by Justice Scalia (76%), then by the other three conservatives (Roberts, Alito and Thomas), who were all on 72% — another sign of the Court's rightward shift.

The two justices most frequently in agreement were — for the third term out of four — Chief Justice Roberts and Associate Justice Alito. Once again Stevens and Thomas, both Republican appointees, were the two justices who most frequently disagreed — on 54% of the term's non-unanimous cases.

The Roberts Court?

By the end of his fourth term as Chief Justice (2008–09), can John Roberts be said to have put his own mark on the Supreme Court? Is the current Court truly the Roberts Court? Certainly, the Chief Justice was the justice most frequently in the majority in 2007–08. In that term's six landmark decisions, Roberts was on the losing side in two — the death penalty for child rape and detainees' rights at Guantánamo Bay. Anthony Kennedy, meanwhile, was in the majority in all six of the landmark decisions of the 2007–08 term. So if not the Roberts Court, then what?

Writing her annual review of the Court's 2007–08 term in the *New York Times*, Linda Greenhouse concluded that once again it was the Kennedy Court.

> Justice Kennedy, who marked his twentieth anniversary on the Court in February 2008, did not compile quite the pitch-perfect voting record in this term that he had in the last. And his vote was not always essential. Two of the major decisions of the term, in which the Court upheld Kentucky's method of execution by lethal injection and Indiana's law requiring voters to produce photo identification at the polls, were decided by more comfortable margins of 7 to 2 and 6 to 3. [But] Justice Kennedy wrote the majority opinion in the Guantánamo case. He silently joined Justice Scalia's majority opinion in the gun case. He wrote the 5–4 majority opinion in the case that ruled out the death penalty for child rape.

Until her retirement from the Supreme Court in 2006, Justice Sandra Day O'Connor was viewed as the 'swing justice' — the justice who sometimes joined the four conservative judges (Rehnquist, Scalia, Thomas and Kennedy), while at other times joining the four liberals (Stevens, Souter, Ginsburg and Breyer) to decide which way the Court divided in 5–4 decisions. But O'Connor was replaced by Justice Samuel Alito, someone who has thus far developed a much more solidly conservative voting record on the Court than O'Connor. It is now Anthony Kennedy who has emerged as the crucial fifth vote in 5–4 decisions. From a historical viewpoint this is particularly appropriate, for Kennedy's appointment to the Court in 1988 came about as a result of the retirement of another centrist justice, Lewis Powell, who had been appointed back in 1972. In his excellent book *Closed Chambers: The Rise, Fall, and Future of the Modern Supreme Court* (Penguin, 1998), Edward Lazarus has this to say of Justice Powell:

> Powell was liked and admired [because of] the crucial role he played on a fiercely divided Court. Shortly before Powell's [retirement] announcement, a leading civil liberties lawyer had called him 'the most powerful man in America.' And with good reason. By any number of statistical measures, Powell was the most important Justice on the Court. He was in the majority more often than any of his colleagues... Even more important, Powell was consistently the 'swing' Justice on a Court that divided 5–4 with unprecedented frequency.

In 2008, Anthony Kennedy celebrated 20 years on the Supreme Court and at 72, he could well serve another decade or more. Lazarus's epitaph for Powell looks like becoming that of his successor too — 'the most important Justice on the Court'.

Questions

1 Why did the Supreme Court uphold Indiana's voter identification law?
2 Explain why the Supreme Court struck down the so-called 'millionaire's amendment' in the McCain–Feingold law.
3 How did the *Davis* decision show the significance of the replacement of Justice Sandra O'Connor by Justice Samuel Alito?
4 What are the two views of the Second Amendment's right 'to keep and bear arms'? Which groups and people support each of the views?
5 Which side of the argument triumphed in the *Heller* decision?
6 What are the likely results of the *Heller* decision?
7 What did the Court decide about the death penalty in the *Baze* v *Rees* and *Kennedy* v *Louisiana* decisions?
8 In what ways did the majority of the Court disagree with the views of President Bush in the *Boumediene* decision?
9 What did the Court say about the white New Haven firefighters' rights in the *Ricci* decision in 2009?
10 What conclusions can be drawn from the statistics and information presented in Table 2.2?
11 Who might be described today as 'the most important Justice on the Court'? Why is this the case?

Chapter 3

The Sotomayor nomination

What you need to know

- The United States Supreme Court is made up of nine justices; one chief justice and eight associate justices.
- Nominations to the Court are made by the president, with the advice and consent of the Senate.
- Appointments to the Court are for life.
- For this reason, the president can make a nomination only upon the death or voluntary resignation of a member of the Court.
- On average, appointments are made approximately every 2 years.

The vacancy

President George W. Bush waited over 4 years to make his first nomination to the United States Supreme Court, but President Obama had to wait only 4 months. On 1 May 2009, Associate Justice David Souter wrote a brief letter to the President indicating his intention to retire from the Supreme Court at the end of its 2008–09 session. Appointed to the Court in 1990 by President George H. W. Bush, Souter had thus served just short of 19 years.

A little over 3 weeks later, President Obama announced that he was nominating Judge Sonia Sotomayor (pronounced *So-toe-my-yore*) of New York, a federal appeal court judge, to replace Justice Souter. Obama had made no secret of his wish to appoint a woman to the Court. Between 1993 and 2005, there were two women serving on the Supreme Court — Sandra Day O'Connor (appointed by President Reagan in 1981) and Ruth Bader Ginsburg (appointed by President Clinton in 1993). In 2005, O'Connor retired and was replaced by Samuel Alito, thus reducing the number of women on the Court to one. Sotomayor's nomination also allowed Obama to appoint the first Hispanic member of the Supreme Court. She was the fourth woman to be nominated following O'Connor, Ginsburg and Harriet Miers — the latter nominated by George W. Bush in 2005, but not confirmed by the Senate.

From the Bronx to the bench

Sotomayor turned 55 just after her nomination and is 7 months older than Chief Justice John Roberts, who will still be the youngest member of the current Court. Her parents arrived in the United States from Puerto Rico, and she and her younger brother were brought up in the Bronx in New York City. Her father died when she was just 9. Having attended New York public (i.e. state) school, she won a scholarship to Princeton University and afterwards went on to Yale Law School, from which she graduated in 1979.

The next 12 years were spent as a lawyer in New York until in 1991 she was nominated by President George H. W. Bush as a judge on the US District Court. Six years later, President Bill Clinton nominated her to the US Court of Appeals, and she was confirmed by the Senate on that occasion by 67 votes to 29.

While much press comment was given to her gender and race, little was made of the fact that Sotomayor becomes the sixth Catholic on the current Court — joining Antonin Scalia, Anthony Kennedy, Clarence Thomas, John Roberts and Samuel Alito. This also makes her the third Catholic in succession to join the Court but the first to be appointed by a Democrat president for over 60 years. Indeed, there have only ever been 12 Catholics on the Court in its entire history, but it just so happens that six of them are now serving together. Given that both Bill Clinton's Supreme Court nominees — Ruth Bader Ginsburg and Stephen Breyer — are Jewish, only one current member of the Court is a protestant Christian — John Paul Stevens, who turns 90 in April of this year.

Republicans' caution

The Sotomayor nomination was generally well received — certainly by Democrats and also by a number of prominent Republicans. Indeed, Republicans were eager not to be seen as anti-Hispanic — Hispanics being a critically important ethnic group whose support George W. Bush had done much to woo during his presidency. 'I think Republicans will oppose her at their peril', remarked Democrat senator Charles Schumer of New York, adding:

> In a certain sense, this is a referendum on the future of the Republican Party, because she is a moderate, and they're going to have real difficulty opposing her. And if you let the 5 percent at the extreme right oppose her and lead them to oppose her, it's going to hurt them.

Republicans — the minority party by 20 seats in the Senate — also realised that not only would heated opposition to Judge Sotomayor be a tactical mistake, it would also be futile. Sotomayor was given a 'well qualified' rating by the American Bar Association. As the *National Journal* pointed out in its cover story (30 May 2009):

> She's well qualified by judicial standards. She's a historic first, meaning senators want to vote to confirm if they can. She's a she — and plenty of Republican senators have applauded the general goal of seeing a Supreme Court that looks more diverse.

Republicans also realised that having been designated by most neutral commentators as a moderate liberal, Sotomayor was unlikely to change the philosophical makeup of the Court to any significant extent, as the justice she was to replace — David Souter — could also be labelled a moderate liberal. In this sense, like the Roberts for Rehnquist nomination back in 2005, the Sotomayor for Souter nomination was being portrayed as a like-for-like replacement, and therefore less controversial. One former George W. Bush aide was quoted as saying of the Sotomayor nomination:

> Is this the hill on which conservative Republicans die? There's only a downside here, because you're going to antagonise a group [Hispanics] that will be extremely excited about the possibility of representation on the Court, and that same group is currently walking away in droves from the Republican Party.

Obama's precedent

It wasn't just the Senate Republicans who faced a tricky task in the upcoming confirmation process. President Obama had to deal with a couple of difficulties of his own creation. First, in writing about his thoughts on judicial philosophy before he became president, Obama had talked about the importance he placed on 'empathy' when looking for judicial candidates. It's all there in his bestselling memoir, *The Audacity of Hope*. This could be seen as something of a hostage to fortune. Many would argue that 'empathy' is not an attribute of any relevance in the courtroom, where justice should be pursued with utter impartiality.

Second, Obama had set an unfortunate precedent when, as the junior senator from Illinois, he voted against the nominations of both John Roberts and Samuel Alito to the Supreme Court. During the Senate floor debate on Roberts's nomination in 2005, Senator Obama had stated: 'There is absolutely no doubt in my mind Judge Roberts is qualified to sit on the highest court in the land.' But he still voted 'no', unlike half of his Democrat colleagues, who voted 'yes'. Senator Obama therefore cast his vote not on judicial qualification, but on political philosophy and expediency — partisan considerations that had nothing to do with the merits of the nominee. Judge Roberts was a conservative, and voting for a conservative on the Supreme Court would make it difficult for Obama to secure the Democratic nomination for the presidency 3 years later.

Now President Obama was telling senators of both parties that they should support Judge Sotomayor because of her outstanding qualifications. He would find his words quoted back at him during the upcoming confirmation hearings.

The Senate's hearings

Judge Sotomayor's confirmation hearings opened in the Senate Judiciary Committee on Monday 13 July, 42 days after her nomination — pretty much par for the course. Since 1975, there has been an average of 31 days between the nomination of a justice for the Supreme Court and the beginning of the hearings on Capitol Hill. During that period, the longest wait was for Robert Bork in 1987 (76 days) and the shortest for John Roberts (6 days). (Roberts, however, had been nominated as an associate justice 2 months earlier, but was later nominated as chief justice on the death of the then chief justice William Rehnquist, just 6 days before the confirmation hearings were due to open.)

What one needs to remember about the Senate confirmation hearings for Supreme Court justices is that, contrary to popular belief, this is not an opportunity to hear the nominee *answer* questions. Rather, it is designed almost entirely for senators to be heard *asking* questions! Nominees make a huge mistake if they think that they are going to be speaking for even 50% of the hearings. It's more a case of 80–20 — 80% of the time being taken up with senators speaking, and a mere 20% of the time left for the nominee to speak. It's hardly surprising that confirmation hearings offer little insight into the nominee themselves.

The Senate Judiciary Committee has changed somewhat in party balance and membership since the Roberts and Alito hearings in 2005 and 2006. Back then, the Republicans held a 2-seat majority on the 18-member committee, with 10 Republicans and 8 Democrats. Now the Democrats have a 5-seat majority on the 19-member committee, with 12 Democrats and just 7 Republicans. Five new Democrat senators have joined the committee since the last hearings. The former Republican chairman of the committee, Arlen Specter of Pennsylvania, now sits as a Democrat, having switched parties in mid-2009.

The hearings opened with introductory statements from the senators and the nominee. Senator Charles Schumer, Sotomayor's home-state senator, choked up with emotion as he retold her life story — the daughter of Puerto Rican immigrants, who grew up in a Bronx public housing project. Committee chairman Patrick Leahy compared Sotomayor's nomination as the first Hispanic on the Court to that of Louis Brandeis, the first Jewish justice, and to Thurgood Marshall, the first African American.

Such controversy as there was surrounding Judge Sotomayor's nomination centred mostly upon a remark she made in a lecture in 2001 at the University of California (Berkeley) Law School, which was published the same year in the Law School's journal:

> I would hope that a wise Latina woman with the richness of her experiences
> would more often than not reach a better conclusion than a white male who
> hasn't lived that life.

Democrats were concerned enough about the remark to give her an opportunity early in the hearings to step away from it. In reply to a question from the committee chairman, Patrick Leahy, Judge Sotomayor stated:

> No words I have ever spoken or written have received so much attention.
> I want to state up front, unequivocally and without doubt: I do not believe
> that any ethnic, racial or gender group has an advantage in sound judging.

Indeed, in asking his question, Senator Leahy misquoted Judge Sotomayor's 'wise Latina woman' comment by omitting the words 'a better conclusion than a white male' and inserting in their place the much more neutral phrase 'wise decisions'. In answer to other questions, Judge Sotomayor went on to suggest that her 'wise Latina woman' remark had been a poor choice of words, a verbal flourish that had fallen flat and that 'the context of the words [had] created a misunderstanding.'

The other matter upon which critics focused was the fact that just a few weeks prior to the Senate hearings, the United States Supreme Court had overturned a decision in which Judge Sotomayor had concurred as an appellate judge. In *Ricci* v *DeStefano*, the US Court of Appeals had agreed with a lower court ruling to disregard the test results for the promotion of firefighters in New Haven, Connecticut, because no African Americans had been promoted as a result of the tests. (A detailed study of the case can be found in Chapter 2.) But in a 5–4 decision, the Supreme Court overturned the lower court rulings with some ensuing embarrassment to Judge Sotomayor, who had signed up to the appeal court's ruling.

In one of the only moments of genuine interest during the hearings, Judge Sotomayor distanced herself from President Obama's oft-stated philosophy that Supreme Court justices should be guided by 'empathy' and their 'hearts' in deciding cases. According to Judge Sotomayor:

> I wouldn't approach the issue of judging the way the President does. Judges
> can't rely on what's in their heart. The job of a judge is to apply the law.

Here was another possible nail in the coffin for the oft-repeated argument that suggests Supreme Court justices are merely echo chambers of the presidents that appoint them. Or was Judge Sotomayor merely playing to the gallery?

On 28 July, the committee voted to recommend Judge Sotomayor for appointment to the Supreme Court by a vote of 13–6. Republican senator Lindsey Graham joined all 12 committee Democrats to vote in favour, while the remaining 6 Republicans voted 'no'.

Sotomayor's confirmation

When he nominated Sotomayor back in May, President Obama had asked the Senate to confirm her nomination in time for the Court's new session beginning in the autumn, and that the Senate duly did. The Senate finally voted on 6 August by a vote of 68–31 to confirm Judge Sotomayor as the 111th justice of the Supreme Court. (The vote was almost identical to the 67–29 vote back in 1997, which confirmed her nomination to the US Court of Appeals.) The whole process from nomination to confirmation had taken 66 days — not far off the average of 60 days during the past 35 years. Table 3.1 shows that her confirmation was nowhere near as speedy as that of John Paul Stevens or John Roberts, but certainly quicker than that of Clarence Thomas and Antonin Scalia.

Table 3.1 Days from nomination to confirmation of Supreme Court justices: 1975–2009

Justice	Nominated by	Year	Days from nomination to confirmation
John Paul Stevens	Ford	1975	19
Sandra O'Connor	Reagan	1981	33
Antonin Scalia	Reagan	1986	85
Anthony Kennedy	Reagan	1988	65
David Souter	Bush (41)	1990	69
Clarence Thomas	Bush (41)	1991	99
Ruth Bader Ginsburg	Clinton	1993	50
Stephen Breyer	Clinton	1994	73
John Roberts	Bush (43)	2005	23
Samuel Alito	Bush (43)	2006	82
Sonia Sotomayor	Obama	2009	66

The 68 'yes' votes were cast by 57 Democrats, 2 Independents and 9 Republicans, while the remaining 31 Republicans voted 'no'. Two Democrats, 91-year-old Robert Byrd of West Virginia and Barbara Mikulski of Maryland, arrived in the chamber in wheelchairs to cast their 'yes' votes. Byrd had been absent from the Senate for much of 2009 due to illness, while Mikulski had just returned from hospital following surgery on a broken ankle. Democrat Ted Kennedy, however, was too ill to vote. Sotomayor's confirmation was therefore more bipartisan than that for Bush appointee Justice Alito in 2006, who was supported by only 4 Democrats, but it was not as bipartisan as the vote for Chief Justice Roberts in 2005, who received 'yes' votes from 22 Democrats. Significantly, none of the 9 Republicans who voted 'yes' on the Sotomayor nomination are standing for re-election in 2010, and 6 of them come from states which voted for Obama in 2008 — Collins and Snowe from Maine, Gregg from New Hampshire, Lugar from Indiana, Martinez from Florida, and Voinovich from Ohio. The only Republican senator from a state which Obama won in 2008 and who voted 'no' was Charles Grassley of Iowa.

The Sotomayor nomination is unlikely to change the ideological balance of the Court — the switch of Sotomayor for Souter is one liberal for another. Given that the next most likely retirees from the Court are also liberal justices — John Paul Stevens and Ruth Bader Ginsburg — future Obama nominations are also unlikely to be ideologically significant.

Questions

1 Why was it unsurprising that President Obama nominated a woman to fill this Supreme Court vacancy?
2 What was remarkable about Judge Sotomayor's upbringing, race and religion?
3 Why were Republicans cautious of criticising Judge Sotomayor too harshly?
4 What two difficulties had President Obama created for himself in the confirmation of Judge Sotomayor?
5 How had the makeup of the Senate Judiciary Committee changed since 2006?
6 What was the controversial remark made by Judge Sotomayor in 2001? How did Judge Sotomayor reply to questions about this remark during the Senate hearings?
7 In what way did Judge Sotomayor disagree with the views of President Obama?
8 To what extent were (a) the vote in the Senate Judiciary Committee and (b) the vote on the Senate floor party-line votes?
9 Why is the Sotomayor nomination unlikely to change the ideological balance of the Supreme Court?
10 Why are future Obama Supreme Court nominations also unlikely to change this balance?

Chapter 4

The 2008 congressional elections

What you need to know

- Congressional elections are held every 2 years.
- At each election, the whole of the House of Representatives and one-third of the Senate are up for re-election.
- Senators serve 6-year terms, with one-third of them subject to re-election every 2 years.
- The senators up for re-election in 2008 were therefore those who were last elected in 2002.

In a presidential election year, the races for the House of Representatives and the Senate tend to take something of a back seat. This was also the case in our 2009 *Annual Survey* where, due to a lack of space, we had to drop the chapter on the most recent set of congressional elections. So here it is, a touch later than usual. As there are no more congressional elections until November 2010 (see Chapter 6), this is still very relevant to our study of current US politics.

At the start of this election cycle, the Democrats controlled both Houses of Congress and no one seriously expected them to lose that control. Indeed, most pundits were forecasting that they would make significant gains in both houses, thereby increasing the majorities they had gained in the 2006 mid-term elections. To what extent did this occur?

The primaries

Four House members were defeated in the 2008 congressional primaries — three Republicans and one Democrat. First to fall were two House members from Maryland — Democrat Albert Wynn in Maryland's 4th congressional district and Republican Wayne Gilchrest in the 1st district. Both incumbents lost their primaries in large part because their constituents perceived them as being out of alignment with the majority of their party. Both Wynn and Gilchrest were senior members of the House. Wynn was first elected in 1992 and had served 8 terms; Gilchrest was first elected in 1990 and had completed 9 terms. Wynn was defeated by Donna Edwards, who accused Wynn of being too conservative for a district in which 78% had voted for John Kerry in 2004. Gilchrest was defeated by Andy Harris, who accused Gilchrest of being too liberal. Both were out of step with their party's position

on the Iraq war, and this brought upon them the ire of primary voters. Wynn was criticised by Edwards for voting for the 2002 resolution that authorised President Bush to use military force in Iraq. Gilchrest was opposed by Harris for being one of only two Republicans who in 2007 supported a Democratic-sponsored measure that would have required President Bush to set a timetable to withdraw troops from Iraq. Edwards held the seat for the Democrats in the general election, while Harris lost in a cliffhanger by around 2,000 out of the approximately 350,000 votes that were cast.

The third House member to lose his seat in a congressional primary in 2008 was Republican Chris Cannon in Utah's 3rd district. Cannon had represented the solidly Republican district since 1996. He was accused of not being conservative enough, and was specifically targeted for supporting a 2002 law that expanded the federal government's oversight of local schools and a 2003 law that added prescription drugs to the benefits offered by the Medicare programme. The winner of the Republican primary — a political novice by the name of Jason Chaffetz — went on to hold the seat for the Republicans in the general election with 66% of the vote.

The fourth primary defeat was something of a surprise — David Davis in Tennessee's 1st congressional district. Pre-election polls showed Davis with a comfortable lead, but in the end he lost the 7 August primary to Johnson City mayor Phil Roe by a handful of votes. Tennessee has an open primary system and Davis's team believed that Democrats, knowing they could not defeat him in the November election, crossed over to defeat him in the Republican primary. Roe held the seat for the Republicans with 72% of the vote in November.

There were, as usual, no defeats in the Senate primaries. Table 4.1 shows that these primary defeats in the House were pretty much in line with those in previous election cycles.

Table 4.1 House and Senate incumbents defeated in primaries: 1988–2008

Year	House members defeated in primaries	Senators defeated in primaries
1988	1	0
1990	1	0
1992	19	1
1994	4	0
1996	2	1
1998	1	0
2000	3	0
2002	8	1
2004	2	0
2006	2	1
2008	4	0

The Senate

In the Senate (see Table 4.2), the party balance before these elections was 49 Democrats and 49 Republicans, plus 2 independents who both lined up with the Democrats, giving the Democrats a 51–49 seat majority. The seats up for election in 2008 were those last contested in 2002, a year in which the Republicans, with a popular president, were riding high. As a consequence,

Table 4.2 Results of Senate elections, 2008

State	Winner	Party	%	Opponent	Party	%
Alabama	**Jeff Sessions**	Rep	63	Vivian Figures	D	37
Alaska	Mark Begich	D	48	**Ted Stevens**	Rep	47
Arkansas	**Mark Pryor**	D	79	Rebekah Kennedy	Green	21
Colorado	Mark Udall	D	52	Bob Schaffer	*Rep	43
Delaware	**Joseph Biden**	D	65	Christine O'Donnell	Rep	35
Georgia	**Saxby Chambliss**	Rep	57	Jim Martin	D	43
Idaho	Jim Risch	*Rep	58	Larry LaRocco	D	34
Illinois	**Richard Durbin**	D	67	Steve Sauerberg	Rep	29
Iowa	**Tom Harkin**	D	63	Chris Reed	Rep	37
Kansas	**Pat Roberts**	Rep	60	Jim Slattery	D	37
Kentucky	**Mitch McConnell**	Rep	53	Greg Fischer	D	47
Louisiana	**Mary Landrieu**	D	52	John Kennedy	Rep	46
Maine	**Susan Collins**	Rep	61	Tom Allen	D	39
Massachusetts	**John Kerry**	D	66	Jeff Beatty	Rep	31
Michigan	**Carl Levin**	D	62	Jack Hoogendyk	Rep	34
Minnesota	Al Franken	D	42	**Norm Coleman**	Rep	42
Mississippi	**Thad Cochran**	Rep	62	Erik Fleming	D	38
Mississippi	**Tom Wicker**	Rep	55	Ronnie Musgrove	D	45
Montana	**Max Baucus**	D	73	Bob Kelleher	Rep	27
Nebraska	Mike Johanns	*Rep	58	Scott Kleeb	D	40
New Hampshire	Jeanne Shaheen	D	52	**John Sununu**	Rep	45
New Jersey	**Frank Lautenberg**	D	55	Dick Zimmer	Rep	43
New Mexico	Tom Udall	D	61	Steve Pearce	*Rep	39
North Carolina	Kay Hagen	D	53	**Elizabeth Dole**	Rep	44
Oklahoma	**James Inhofe**	Rep	57	Andrew Rice	D	39
Oregon	Jeff Merkley	D	49	**Gordon Smith**	Rep	46
Rhode Island	**Jack Reed**	D	73	Bob Tingle	Rep	27
South Carolina	**Lindsey Graham**	Rep	58	Bob Conley	D	42
South Dakota	**Tim Johnson**	D	62	Joel Dykstra	Rep	38
Tennessee	**Lamar Alexander**	Rep	65	Bob Tuke	D	31
Texas	**John Cornyn**	Rep	55	Rick Noriega	D	43
Virginia	Mark Warner	D	64	James Gilmore	*Rep	35
West Virginia	**John Rockefeller**	D	64	Jay Wolfe	Rep	36
Wyoming	**Michael Enzi**	Rep	76	Chris Rothfuss	D	24
Wyoming	**John Barrasso**	Rep	73	Nick Carter	D	27

Incumbents in bold

* Open seat: party controlling seat before election

the majority of seats in these elections — 23 of the 35 — were being defended by the Republicans. Pressure was further put on the Republicans by the fact that five Republican senators announced their retirement, whereas there were no Democrat retirees. Of the five open seats these retirements caused, the Republicans would lose three.

The Republicans lost two long-serving senators by retirement — John Warner in Virginia and Pete Domenici in New Mexico. Both Virginia and New Mexico are becoming progressively blue states, and both were won by Barack Obama in the presidential race. Couple that with the fact that the Democrats recruited very strong candidates for both races, and you had a recipe for Republican losses. In Virginia, the popular former governor Mark Warner — no relation of John Warner — won easily by 64–35. So Virginia, which as recently as 2006 had two Republican senators, is now represented by two Democratic senators. In New Mexico, Democrat Congressman Tom Udall easily saw off Republican Congressman Steve Pearce, 61–39. Meanwhile, Tom Udall's cousin Mark won an open seat in Colorado, this one caused by the retirement of the two-term Republican Wayne Allard.

As well as the loss of these three open seats, the Republicans lost five incumbents — Ted Stevens in Alaska, John Sununu in New Hampshire, Gordon Smith in Oregon, Elizabeth Dole in North Carolina and Norm Coleman in Minnesota — giving a total of eight losses for the Republican Party.

Ted Stevens was appointed to the Senate in 1968 and elected to his first full term in 1972. In his 40 years as a senator — an all-time record for a Republican — he had never been re-elected with less than 66% of the vote. In 2002, he was re-elected to his sixth term with 78% of the vote. However, the 84-year-old Stevens was under federal investigation for much of 2008 on seven counts of felony and financial deception. Then, just a week before election day, he was convicted in a Washington courtroom on all seven counts. That should have finished any chance Stevens might have had for a seventh term, but he was only narrowly defeated by Anchorage Mayor Mark Begich. Begich was just 6 years old when Stevens began his senate career!

John Sununu faced a rematch of his 2002 race against the popular former governor of New Hampshire, Jeanne Shaheen. Whereas 6 years earlier, with the fortunes of President Bush and the Republican Party running high, he had defeated her 51–46, this time around he lost 45–52. Like Sununu, Gordon Smith found himself to be a Republican swimming against the tide in a blue state, and lost his re-election bid to the Speaker of the Oregon House of Representatives, Jeff Merkley.

The loss Republicans felt most keenly was that of Elizabeth Dole in North Carolina. Liddy Dole is the wife of the former Kansas Republican senator and 1996 presidential candidate Bob Dole. She served as transportation secretary to Ronald Reagan and as labor secretary to George H. W. Bush. She has also been president of the American Red Cross. Dole was first elected to the Senate in 2002, when she comfortably defeated the former Clinton White House Chief of Staff Erskine Bowles by 54–45. When in 2008 prominent Democrats such as former North Carolina governor James Hunt declined to challenge her, Senator Dole looked like a safe bet for re-election — the more so when a little-known state senator, Kay Hagen, won the Democratic primary. However, Dole eventually ran foul of her wholehearted support of President Bush, her failure to look after the interests of North Carolinians, and Barack Obama's decision to campaign aggressively in the state. She ended up losing 44–53.

Republicans lost the senate race in Minnesota by a hair's breadth, with incumbent Norm Coleman falling to his Democrat challenger Al Franken by fewer than 200 votes out of almost 3 million. The race was complicated by three third party candidates, one of which — Dean Barkley of the Minnesota Independence Party — gained over 15% of the vote. The recounting and court challenges went on for over 6 months, meaning that Franken did not take up his seat in the Senate until May 2009. The Republicans, who lost six incumbent senators in the mid-term elections of 2006, had now lost another five in 2008.

Something that was evident in both the Senate and House races in 2008 was how vulnerable Republicans tried to save their seats by moving away, politically, from an unpopular president in their re-election year. Take Gordon Smith, for example. In the whole 8 years of the Bush era, Smith had an 80% support score of the President. But if one looks at 2008 alone, his support score was just 45%. The same went for Elizabeth Dole, for whom an 87% support score in 2001–08 fell to just 53% in 2008. Both lost their seats. For Dole, her closeness to President Bush was used very effectively in television ads put out by the Democratic Senatorial Campaign Committee (DSCC) in support of her opponent, Kay Hagen. Here's how one DSCC ad went:

> 1965 — the Beatles were new, Lyndon Johnson was president, and Elizabeth Dole moved to Washington. Forty-three years later, what's she been doing? Voting with George Bush 92 percent of the time: against increasing the minimum wage; for tax breaks that export jobs; for tax breaks for big oil. Elizabeth Dole — just not getting the job done.

Other Republican senators who tried to walk away from the President in election year included Norm Coleman of Minnesota, Ted Stevens of Alaska and Saxby Chambliss of Georgia. All had a significantly lower support scores for President Bush in 2008 than during the rest of his presidency.

Third party candidates made little or no impact on most congressional races, other than the senate race in Minnesota, displaying yet again the dominance of the two major parties. In the race for the senate seat in Arkansas, the Green

Party candidate won 21% of the vote, but there was no Republican candidate in the race, Democrat Mark Pryor winning re-election with 79% of the vote. In Tennessee, third parties need only 25 signatures to get their name on the ballot, and as usual many races in the state featured multiple candidates. Lamar Alexander, the Republican senator seeking re-election, found himself with seven opponents, but still managed to win 65% of the vote. Twenty-five of the 30 senators who sought re-election in 2008 were indeed re-elected. Table 4.3 shows that the 83.3% re-election rate is very similar to re-election rates in recent election cycles.

Table 4.3 Senators: retired, defeated, re-elected, 1988–2008

Year	Retired	Sought re-election	Defeated in primary	Defeated in general election	Total re-elected	% re-elected who sought re-election
1988	6	27	0	4	23	85.2
1990	3	32	0	1	31	96.9
1992	7	28	1	4	23	82.1
1994	9	26	0	2	24	92.3
1996	13	21	1	1	19	90.5
1998	5	29	0	3	26	89.6
2000	5	29	0	5	24	82.8
2002	5	28	1	3	24	85.7
2004	8	26	0	1	25	96.1
2006	4	29	1*	6	23	79.3
2008	5	30	0	5	25	83.3

* In 2006, Senator Joe Lieberman (D-Conn) was defeated in the Democratic primary but was then re-elected as an Independent

The eight Republican losses in the 2008 elections were joined by a ninth in April 2009, when Republican senator Arlen Specter of Pennsylvania switched parties to join the Democrats. This gave the Democrats effectively 60 seats in the Senate — the so-called filibuster-proof majority which they had sought.

The House of Representatives

In the final days of this election campaign, the bottom seemed to be falling out of the Republican campaign for the House of Representatives. Having lost 21 seats in 2006, it looked as if they could lose over 30 more in 2008. In the end, the Republican losses were not quite as bad as expected — though they were bad enough — and were slightly offset by the pick-up of four Democrat seats.

Before the elections, the Democrats had 236 House seats and the Republicans 199. Overall, the Republicans lost 14 incumbents and 12 open seats for a total loss of 26 seats, which with the five gains from the Democrats gave them an overall loss of 21 seats. The party balance in the new House of Representatives in January 2009 was therefore 257 Democrats and 178 Republicans. This returned the House to the almost exact party balance it was just before the

1994 mid-term elections: 259–176. It was in 1994 that the Republicans gained over 50 seats and became the majority party in the House for the first time in 40 years.

Table 4.4 House members: retired, defeated, re-elected: 1988–2008

Year	Retired	Sought re-election	Defeated in primary	Defeated in general election	Total re-elected	% re-elected who sought re-election
1988	26	409	1	6	402	98.3
1990	27	407	1	15	391	96.1
1992	67	368	19	24	325	88.3
1994	48	387	4	34	349	90.2
1996	50	383	2	21	360	94.0
1998	33	401	1	6	394	98.3
2000	32	403	3	6	394	97.8
2002	38	397	8	8	381	96.0
2004	29	404	2	7	395	97.8
2006	28	405	2	21	382	94.3
2008	32	402	4	19	379	94.3

Four of the five Democrats defeated were first-term members of the House (see Table 4.5). Indeed, Don Cazayoux had won his House seat in Louisiana only 6 months before, in March 2008, in a special election to fill the vacancy left by the retirement of Republican Richard Baker. Cazayoux had won only 49% of the vote and was vulnerable to the Republicans recapturing the seat straightaway. Nancy Boyda lost her seat in Kansas after just 2 years, having won by the slenderest of margins in 2006. The Republicans also recaptured the seat which until 2006 was held by former House Majority Leader Tom DeLay. After DeLay was embroiled in an ethics scandal, the Democrats won the seat with 52% of the vote. Democrat Nick Lampson lasted just one term.

The most bizarre result was in Florida's 16th district, where the Democrats had made a surprise gain in 2006 after the incumbent Republican, Mark Foley, was caught up in a sex scandal just before the election. The beneficiary was Democrat Tim Mahoney, who won with a mere 50% of the vote in 2006. So what happened in 2008? Like his predecessor, Mahoney was caught in a sex scandal right before the election, and the Republicans won back the seat — with 60% of the vote. Finally, in an election delayed to 5 December, nine-term Democrat William Jefferson (Louisiana 2) lost his bid for re-election after being indicted on federal bribery, racketeering and other corruption charges. The Republican winner in that race, Anh Quang (Joseph) Cao, became the first Vietnamese-American elected to Congress.

Of the 14 Republican House members defeated in 2008, six had been in Congress for 10 years or longer. The longest-serving member to be defeated was moderate Republican Chris Shays in Connecticut. Shays was seeking election to his 12th term, having been re-elected with just 51% of the vote in

Table 4.5 House incumbents defeated in the general election, 2008

House member	Party	Congressional District	First elected
Nancy Boyda	D	Kansas 2	2006
Don Cazayoux	D	Louisiana 6	2008
Steve Chabot	Rep	Ohio 1	1994
Thelma Drake	Rep	Virginia 2	2004
Phil English	Rep	Pennsylvania 3	1994
Tom Feeney	Rep	Florida 24	2002
Virgil Goode	Rep	Virginia 5	1996
Robin Hayes	Rep	North Carolina 8	1998
William Jefferson	D	Louisiana 2	1990
Ric Keller	Rep	Florida 8	2000
Joe Knollenberg	Rep	Michigan 9	1992
John 'Randy' Kuhl	Rep	New York 29	2004
Nick Lampson	D	Texas 22	2006
Tim Mahoney	D	Florida 16	2006
Marilyn Musgrave	Rep	Colorado 4	2002
Jon Porter	Rep	Nevada 3	2002
Bill Sali	Rep	Idaho 1	2006
Christopher Shays	Rep	Connecticut 4	1987
Tim Walberg	Rep	Michigan 7	2006

2006. Shays' defeat means that there are now no Republican House members in any of the six New England states — Maine, Vermont, New Hampshire, Massachusetts, Connecticut or Rhode Island. All 23 House members are now Democrats. Indeed, if you expand that area to include five more states — New York, New Jersey, Pennsylvania, Delaware and Maryland — there are now only 16 Republicans in the House from the northeast, compared with 77 Democrats. Having lost the Solid South, the Democrats now have the Solid Northeast. In those 11 northeastern states, 19 of the senators are also Democrats, with Republican senators in only Maine (2) and New Hampshire. The Republicans have lost 18 House seats from this region in just the last two election cycles, including six in New York and five in Pennsylvania.

Table 4.6 Republican losses in the House by geographic region, 2008

Region	Districts lost by Republicans
Northeast: 7	Connecticut 4
	Maryland 1
	New Jersey 3
	New York 13
	New York 25
	New York 29
	Pennsylvania 3
South: 7	Alabama 2
	Florida 8
	Florida 24
	North Carolina 8

Region	Districts lost by Republicans
	Virginia 2
	Virginia 5
	Virginia 11
Midwest: 6	Colorado 4
	Illinois 11
	Michigan 7
	Michigan 9
	Ohio 1
	Ohio 16
West: 5	Arizona 1
	Idaho 1
	Nevada 3
	New Mexico 1
	New Mexico 2

This decimation of the Republicans in the northeast brings into question how much longer one can talk about Rockefeller Republicans — a term given to moderate Republicans in the northeast. What has happened to the party that gave us not only Nelson Rockefeller in New York but the Bush family dynasty in Connecticut? Moderate Republicans in the northeast have been hurt by the base of the party shifting to the more conservative South and Midwest. At the same time, the Republican Party has moved away from an agenda of *fiscal* conservatism, small government and lower taxes, to a *socially* conservative agenda dominated by such issues as abortion, school prayer and gay marriage. Conservative Republicans from the South began to pour scorn on moderate Republicans such as Senator Lincoln Chafee of Rhode Island (defeated in 2006) and Chris Shays in Connecticut, referring to them as RINOs — Republicans in name only.

Eight of the 14 defeated Republican House members came from states which voted for George W. Bush in 2004 but for Barack Obama in 2008. Two others were from Michigan — the state from which John McCain announced in mid-October that he was withdrawing, in an admission that Obama would win the state.

Table 4.7 shows that five House members tried to run for the Senate in this year, of which two won — the Udall cousins. The senate race in New Mexico shows the extent to which House members regard the Senate as more powerful and prestigious than the House. When Republican senator Pete Domenici announced his retirement, all three New Mexico House members entered their respective party primaries. In the Republican primary, Steve Pearce from New Mexico's 2nd District defeated the 1st District incumbent Heather Wilson. Meanwhile, the incumbent Democrat from the state's 3rd District, Tom Udall, captured his party's nomination in the Democrat primary. Thus all three New Mexico House members are new in 2009.

Table 4.7 House members seeking other elective offices, 2008

House member	Party	State/CD	Running for	Result
Tom Allen	D	Maine 1	Senate	Lost
Kenny Hulshof	Rep	Missouri 9	Governor	Lost
Duncan Hunter	Rep	California 52	President	Withdrew
Steve Pearce	Rep	New Mexico 2	Senate	Lost
Tom Tancredo	Rep	Colorado 6	President	Withdrew
Mark Udall	D	Colorado 2	Senate	Won
Tom Udall	D	New Mexico 3	Senate	Won
Heather Wilson	Rep	New Mexico 1	Senate	Lost

Figure 4.1 shows that just 61 districts were won with less than 55% of the vote — that is, they were decided by less than 10% of the vote, making them truly competitive. From a high point of 111 competitive districts in 1992, this number shrank to just 31 by 2004. In 2006 the number rose to 58, and it rose again to 61 in 2008. However, it still means that 374 districts (86%) are safe for one of the two major parties. Indeed, in 28 districts there was no contest at all, as only one party fielded a candidate.

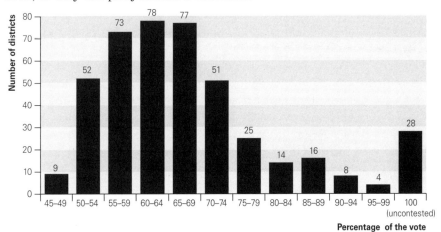

Figure 4.1 Percentage of the vote for winning House candidates, 2008

Conclusions

The makeup of the new 111th Congress, which began in January 2009, looked politically quite different from its predecessor. There were significantly more Democrats in both chambers. In other respects, though, the two chambers looked much the same. The number of women was up from 71 to 75 in the House and from 16 to 17 in the Senate — all-time highs. The vast majority of women in both chambers are Democrats: 58 out of 75 in the House and 13 out of 17 in the Senate. In the Senate, the Republicans lost Elizabeth Dole (North Carolina) while the Democrats gained Kay Hagen (North Carolina) and Jeanne Shaheen (New Hampshire).

In terms of race, both chambers look very much as they did before. The number of African Americans in the House fell to 39 — all of whom are Democrats. Meanwhile, Barack Obama — the Senate's only black member — resigned on 16 November 2008. He was controversially replaced by Roland Burris — another African-American — who was nominated to fill the vacancy by Illinois governor Rod Blagojevich, just before the governor was impeached and removed from office by the Illinois state legislature. Burris announced some months later that he would not defend the seat in 2010. (This is discussed in more detail in Chapter 7.) The number of Hispanics in the House increased by 1 to 24 — 21 of whom are Democrats — and remained at three in the Senate (that is, until Senator Mel Martinez (R–Florida) resigned later in 2009), two of these being Democrats.

The years of the 111th Congress (2009–10) featured united government — a Democrat president with Democrat majorities in both houses of Congress. In the 32 years between 1969 and 2001, there was united government in Washington for only 6 years. Divided government was very much the order of the day. Now, in the 12 years between 2001 and 2013, there are likely to be $8^1/_2$ years of united government.

Questions

1 What was the common factor in the defeat of Maryland congressmen Albert Wynn (D) and Wayne Gilchrest (R) in their respective 2008 primaries?
2 Why was Chris Cannon (R–Utah) defeated in his 2008 primary?
3 What factors led to the defeat of David Davis (R–Tenn) in his primary?
4 What two factors led to the Republicans losing the Senate seats in Virginia, New Mexico and Colorado?
5 What factors led to the defeat of Ted Stevens (R–Alaska) after 40 years in the Senate?
6 What effect did outgoing president George W. Bush have on the 2008 congressional races?
7 What effect did third parties have on the 2008 congressional elections?
8 What was the common factor among four of the five House Democrats who were defeated in 2008?
9 What has happened to the Republican Party in the northeast in recent congressional elections?
10 What did the Senate race in New Mexico in 2008 tell us about how much many House members covet a seat in the Senate?
11 What does Figure 4.1 show us concerning how competitive the House elections were in 2008?
12 Comment on the makeup of the 111th Congress (2009–10) in terms of party, gender and race.

Chapter 5

The Electoral College, split-ticket voting and coattails in 2008

We gave over the whole of the 2009 *Annual Survey* to an account and analysis of the 2008 presidential election. Since that was published, further data have become available that give us more insight into the election and allow us to update our knowledge and understanding of three aspects of American elections: the workings of the Electoral College, split-ticket voting and the so-called 'coattails effect'.

The Electoral College

What you need to know

- The Electoral College is the mechanism by which the president is elected.
- Each state has a number of Electoral College votes equal to its total representation in Congress, i.e. senators (2) plus members of the House of Representatives.
- The candidate who wins the popular vote in a state wins all the Electoral College votes of that state — except in Maine and Nebraska.
- There are 538 Electoral College votes in all.
- To win the presidency, a candidate needs to win an absolute majority of the Electoral College votes — that is, at least 270.

Forty-eight of the fifty states allocate their Electoral College votes on a winner-takes-all basis. Only Maine and Nebraska do not, choosing instead to allocate one Electoral College vote to the winner in each congressional district within the state, and then awarding the remaining two Electoral College votes to the state-wide winner. In 2008, this resulted in Nebraska awarding 4 votes to John McCain and 1 to Barack Obama. McCain won the popular vote in two of Nebraska's districts while Obama won the remaining district, with McCain winning the state-wide vote. Under the current arrangements, Obama beat McCain in the Electoral College by 365 votes to 173. But what if all 50 states adopted the Maine and Nebraska system for allocating Electoral College votes?

The answer is that Obama would still have won the election, but it would have been much closer than under the current system. The analysis of district-by-district voting in the 2008 presidential race found that Barack Obama won in 242 congressional districts while John McCain carried the remaining 193. In terms of states won, Obama won in 28 states with McCain winning 22. That would give Obama another 56 Electoral College votes and McCain a further 44. Add 3 to Obama's total for winning the District of Columbia, and you get the totals of: Obama 301; McCain 237.

In the popular vote, Obama won 53% to McCain's 46%. In the Electoral College, Obama's 365 votes represented 68% to McCain's 32%, a significant distortion in favour of the winner — a frequent occurrence, some would say a weakness, of the current winner-takes-all Electoral College system. The 301–237 split in the Electoral College vote would have represented a 56%–44% split between Obama and McCain, much closer to the popular vote than the winner-takes-all system. The reason for the discrepancy in the winner-takes-all system in 2008 was that Obama dominated the vote in the most populous states but won his districts more overwhelmingly than did McCain. Therefore the district-based system — as used in Maine and Nebraska — would have been less favourable to Obama, because his supermajorities in many districts would have been wasted surpluses.

The district-based plan would certainly have more fairly represented McCain's success in a state like Florida. Because Obama won the state — by just 3 percentage points — he won all the 27 Electoral College votes of Florida. However, although Obama won state-wide, McCain won 15 of the state's 25 districts, so under a district-based plan, McCain would have won 15 Electoral College votes to Obama's 12. A similar result would have occurred in North Carolina, Ohio and Pennsylvania — all states where Obama won state-wide but won fewer districts than McCain.

Split-ticket voting

Conventional wisdom has it that split-ticket voting has declined in recent decades. This is where voters vote for candidates of different parties for different offices at the same election — for example, voting for a Democrat president but a Republican congressman. To what extent was the conventional wisdom proved correct in 2008?

In 2008, there were 83 congressional districts in which voters split their tickets — voting either Democrat for president but Republican for the House, or Republican for president but Democrat for the House. Thus in the House in 2009–10, there are what we might call 34 'Obama-Republicans' and 49 'McCain-Democrats'. Many of these 83 districts will become the battleground for control of the House of Representatives in the 2010 mid-term House elections.

Table 5.1 shows that while the figure of 83 split districts is a significant increase on the 2004 figure of 59, it is still the second lowest since 1952, thereby supporting the conventional wisdom that split-ticket voting has significantly declined over the past two decades. In 1984, 44% of House districts split their vote between the presidency and the House of Representatives; in 2008, that figure was just 19%. Whether the 2004 figure will prove to be a low-water mark, or the 2008 figure will merely be a blip, is yet to be seen.

Table 5.1 Number of split districts in presidential election years, 1952–2008

Year	Number of split districts
1952	84
1956	130
1960	114
1964	145
1968	139
1972	192
1976	124
1980	143
1984	190
1988	148
1992	100
1996	110
2000	86
2004	59
2008	83

The Obama-Republicans

By Obama-Republicans we mean Republican House members whose districts voted for Barack Obama in 2008. Do these 34 Obama-Republicans have any particular characteristics? First, they are mostly incumbents; only three of them are freshmen (first-term members) — Anh 'Joseph' Cao (Louisiana's 2nd District), Erik Paulsen (Minnesota's 3rd District), and Leonard Lance (New Jersey's 7th District). Second, the 31 incumbents are mostly moderate or 'centrist' Republicans. Of the nine incumbent Republicans in districts which Obama won by 10 percentage points or more, seven are moderate Republicans, including Michael Castle (Delaware At-Large), Mark Kirk (Illinois' 10th District) and Jim Gerlach (Pennsylvania's 6th District), respectively the third, fourth and fifth most moderate Republicans in the House, ranked according to their voting record in 2008. Over one-third of the Obama-Republicans (12 out of 34) come from just two states: eight from California and another four from Obama's home state of Illinois.

These are the House Republicans whom President Obama will want to woo if he is to fulfil his promise of passing bipartisan legislation through Congress. On 5 March 2009, Michael Castle of Delaware was one of seven Republicans to vote in favour of the passage of the Helping Families Save Their Homes Bill. On 26 June 2009, seven of the eight Republicans who voted for the American Clean Energy and Security Bill (commonly known as the Cap-and-Trade Bill) were Obama Republicans.

The McCain-Democrats

By McCain-Democrats we mean Democrat House members whose districts voted for John McCain in 2008. The most notable of these was Gene Taylor (Mississippi 4). While he won re-election as a Democrat with 75% of the vote over his Republican challenger, John McCain carried his district with 68% of the vote. Do these 49 McCain-Democrats have any characteristics in common? Most of them (36 of the 49) are incumbents, but a significant proportion of them (27%) are freshmen. Four of them were elected in districts where John McCain beat Barack Obama by 10 percentage points and more, and who won their own race by a whisker (see Table 5.2). These House members will be the most vulnerable in the 2010 mid-term elections.

Table 5.2 Democrat freshmen narrowly elected in districts where John McCain won by more than 10 percentage points (2008)

House member	District	Margins of victory (in percentage points)	
		John McCain	House member
Bobby Bright	Alabama 2	26	1
Walt Minnick	Idaho 1	26	1
Parker Griffith	Alabama 5	23	3
Frank Kratovil	Maryland 1	18	1

Twenty of these 49 McCain-Democrats (41%) come from the South, including three from both Arkansas and Tennessee. Thirty-two of the 36 incumbent McCain-Democrats (89%) are among the most conservative Democrats in the House, ranked according to their voting record in 2008. Nine of the 12 most conservative Democrats are McCain-Democrats (see Table 5.3). Eight of the McCain-Democrats had no major party opposition in 2008: four were returned unopposed while another four faced only third party opposition.

Table 5.3 Presidential vote in district of 12 most conservative Democrats, 2008

House member	District	% of vote 2008	McCain-Obama vote in district (%)
Jim Marshall	Georgia 8	57	56
Dan Boren	Oklahoma 2	71	66
Brad Ellsworth	Indiana 8	65	51
John Barrow	Georgia 12	66	44
Joe Donnelly	Indiana 2	67	45
Jim Matheson	Utah 2	63	58
Melissa Bean	Illinois 8	60	43
Jason Altmire	Pennsylvania 4	56	55
Christopher Carney	Pennsylvania 10	56	53
Gene Taylor	Mississippi 4	75	67
Baron Hill	Indiana 9	58	50
Heath Shuler	North Carolina 11	62	52

Note: McCain-Democrats in bold

On 26 June 2009, of the 44 Democrats who voted against the passage of the Clean Air Bill, 29 were McCain-Democrats. These 44 Democrats also included 8 of the 12 most conservative Democrats, as shown in Table 5.3.

The coattails effect

The coattails effect is when a strong presidential candidate attracts votes for other candidates of his party standing for other offices at the same election — riding into office, as it were, on his coattails. For there to have been a coattails effect in 2008, we would need to see evidence of Barack Obama helping other Democrats get elected, for example in the House and the Senate. Conventional wisdom tells us that recent incoming presidents have had very little, if any, coattails effect. Indeed, sometimes it has appeared that members of the president's party have got themselves elected *despite*, rather than because of, their association with the president. What was the evidence in 2008?

Obama brought eight new Democrat senators with him to Washington in January 2009, four of them in states that had voted for George W. Bush in 2004 but had switched to Obama in 2008 — Colorado, New Mexico, North Carolina and Virginia. Table 5.4 shows that when compared with his seven immediate predecessors, Obama's success at winning eight Senate seats for his party was a substantial achievement. Indeed, three of Obama's seven immediate predecessors — Kennedy (1960) and both Bushes (1988 and 2000) — actually saw losses for their party in the Senate, and a further two — Jimmy Carter (1980) and Bill Clinton (1992) — made no gains at all. Obama is one of only three presidents in the last 50 years — and the only Democrat — to make gains for his party in the Senate while being elected to his first term in the White House.

Table 5.4 Senate seats gained/lost by incoming president's party, 1960–2008

Year	President	Senate seats gained/lost by incoming president's party
1960	John Kennedy	−2
1968	Richard Nixon	+5
1976	Jimmy Carter	0
1980	Ronald Reagan	+12
1988	George H.W. Bush	−1
1992	Bill Clinton	0
2000	George W. Bush	−4
2008	Barack Obama	+8

However, other evidence points to the lack of a coattails effect for Obama in Senate races. Of the 20 Democrat senators elected on the same ballot, Obama out-polled only five of them, and four of those were freshmen. Admittedly, incumbent members of Congress would often expect to out-poll their party's presidential candidate — they are well known in the state or district, and they often face weak opposition. However, the only incumbent Democrat senator whom Obama out-polled was Frank Lautenberg in New Jersey, where the senator won 55% of the vote and Obama got 57%. On average, Democrat senators who won in 2008 out-polled Obama by just under 8 percentage points, and Mark Pryor of Arkansas out-polled Obama by 40 percentage points! Not much evidence of coattails there.

What about the House races: was there any evidence of Obama coattails for these? As Table 5.5 shows, the Democrats won 21 seats in the House in 2008 — the second best performance by any incoming president in the last 50 years. Indeed, Obama's three immediate predecessors all saw their parties lose seats in the House of Representatives upon their arrival in Washington. In 2008, the Democrats were hoping for more gains in the House — many commentators were predicting at least 30 seats in the days just before the election. Democrat gains were especially marked in states where Obama performed strongly. The Democrats gained three seats in each of New York, Ohio and Virginia, as well as both the open seats in New Mexico.

Table 5.5 House seats gained/lost by incoming president's party, 1960–2008

Year	President	House seats gained/lost by incoming president's party
1960	John Kennedy	−21
1968	Richard Nixon	+3
1976	Jimmy Carter	+2
1980	Ronald Reagan	+33
1988	George H.W. Bush	−3
1992	Bill Clinton	−10
2000	George W. Bush	−2
2008	Barack Obama	+21

Of the 257 Democrats elected to the House of Representatives in the 2008 elections, Barack Obama out-polled just 36 (14%) of them. Of those 36, only 23 were incumbents, the other 13 being freshmen. Furthermore, the number of House Democrats whom Obama out-polled by more than 5 percentage points was just seven, of whom only three were incumbents (see Table 5.6).

Table 5.6 Democrat House members whom Obama out-polled by more than 5 percentage points, 2008

District	House member	House member's % of vote	Obama's % of vote	Obama's percentage-point lead over House member
California 8	Nancy Pelosi	72	85	+13
Connecticut 4	Jim Himes†	51	60	+9
Indiana 7	André Carson	65	71	+6
Maine 1	Chellie Pingree†	55	61	+6
Michigan 13	Carolyn Kilpatrick	74	84	+10
Nevada 3	Dina Titus†	47	55	+8
Ohio 15	Mary Jo Kilroy†	46	54	+8

† Freshman

Another way in which one can look at a possible coattail effect is to gauge the number of congressional districts that the incoming president managed to switch over to his party in the presidential race. Of the 435 congressional districts, 360 of them voted for the presidential candidate of the same party in all three elections of 2000, 2004 and 2008. In other words, they voted either Bush-Bush-McCain or Gore-Kerry-Obama. Of the remaining 75 districts, 52 voted Bush-Bush-Obama in these three elections. Of those 52, nine were in California, seven in Michigan, six in Illinois, and four in Virginia — all states where Obama ran strongly and probably helped to flip these districts from Republican to Democrat in the presidential race. Only one district voted Gore-Kerry-McCain — Pennsylvania's 12th district, which voted 55–44 for Gore in 2000, 51–49 for Kerry in 2004, but 50–49 for McCain in 2008.

So where does all this leave us? The respected political commentator Rhodes Cook ('Obama and the Redefinition of Presidential Coattails', *Rasmussen Reports*, 17 April 2009) had this to say on the matter:

> Barack Obama showed considerable vote-getting ability with a clear-cut win in both the popular and electoral votes. But when it came to presidential coattails, his were of the same modest length of many of his predecessors.

Cook goes on to point out that Obama's ability to out-poll only 36 Democratic House winners pales into insignificance against the coattails of the likes of Eisenhower in 1956, Johnson in 1964 and Nixon in 1972 — all of whom ran ahead of more than 100 victorious House candidates of their own party (see Table 5.7).

Table 5.7 Number of winning House candidates of his party the president out-polled, 1956–2008

Year	Presidential election winner	Popular vote (%)	Number of winning House candidates of his party the president out-polled
1956	Dwight Eisenhower (Rep)	57	155
1964	Lyndon Johnson (D)	61	134
1972	Richard Nixon (Rep)	61	104
1984	Ronald Reagan (Rep)	59	59
2004	George W. Bush (Rep)	51	39
1980	**Ronald Reagan (Rep)**	51	38
2008	**Barack Obama (D)**	53	36
1996	Bill Clinton (D)	49	27
1988	**George H. W. Bush (Rep)**	53	26
2000	**George W. Bush (Rep)**	48	26
1960	**John Kennedy (D)**	50	22
1976	**Jimmy Carter (D)**	50	22
1992	**Bill Clinton (D)**	43	4

Note: first-term presidents in bold

However, Cook's argument is open to two challenges. First, Eisenhower in 1956, Johnson in 1964 and Nixon in 1972 were all incumbent presidents. Second, only one presidential candidate has run ahead of more than 40 House members of his own party since 1972 — and that was Reagan in 1984, another incumbent president. In 1980, as an incoming first-term president, Reagan ran ahead of 38 victorious House Republicans — almost exactly the same as Obama's achievement in 2008. By this measure, Obama performed more strongly than most of his immediate first-term predecessors.

The crunch in presidential coattails comes down to this: are there members of Congress to whom the president can say: 'You probably wouldn't be here today were it not for my helping you get elected in your state or district'? For Barack Obama in 2009 and 2010, there certainly are such Democrats — senators Jeanne Shaheen of New Hampshire, Jeff Merkley of Oregon and Al Franken of Minnesota, and House members such as Mary Jo Kilroy, Dina Titus and Jim Himes. It is worth watching their record of presidential support in the current Congress.

Questions

1 How would the Electoral College result of the 2008 presidential election have been different if all 50 states had cast their Electoral College votes on a district-by-district basis?
2 What is split-ticket voting?
3 What do we mean by Obama-Republicans? What characteristics do many of the Obama-Republicans in the House of Representatives have in common?
4 What do we mean by McCain-Democrats? What characteristics do many of the McCain-Democrats in the House of Representatives have in common?
5 What is the coattails effect?
6 What does Table 5.4 tell us about Obama's coattails effect in the 2008 Senate races?
7 What other evidence points to different conclusions about these Senate races?
8 What does Table 5.5 tell us about Obama's coattails effect in the 2008 House races?
9 What does Rhodes Cook have to say about Obama's coattails effect in 2008?
10 What counter-arguments are suggested to Cook's conclusions in the penultimate paragraph?
11 Give some examples of House and Senate Democrats who probably owe their seats to Barack Obama.

Chapter 6

The 2010 mid-term Congressional elections

What you need to know

- Congressional elections are held every 2 years.
- At each election the whole of the House of Representatives and one-third of the Senate are up for re-election.
- Senators serve 6-year terms, with one-third of them subject to re-election every 2 years.
- The senators up for re-election in 2010 are therefore those who were last elected in 2004.

Overview

The 2010 Congressional elections — to be held on Tuesday 2 November — will fall midway through the presidential term of Barack Obama, hence they are known as mid-term elections. The whole of the House of Representatives and one-third of the Senate will be up for re-election. These senators were elected in 2004, the year of President George W. Bush's re-election, in which the Republicans did quite well, making a net gain of four seats. Of these 34 Senate seats up for re-election, the Republicans currently hold 18 and the Democrats 16.

There will also be special elections in Delaware, New York and Massachusetts — all Democrat-held seats. The seat in Delaware is the one from which Joe Biden resigned after the 2008 presidential election, following his election as vice-president. The seat in New York is the one from which Hillary Clinton resigned when she was appointed secretary of state in January 2009. The seat in Massachusetts was held by Edward Kennedy until his death in August 2009. If Republican senator Kay Bailey Hutchison of Texas should resign in order to run for the state governorship, it would make another senate race. This means there could be an unusually high 38 Senate races in 2010 — 34 for a full 6-year term, two to complete the remaining 4 years of Biden's and Kennedy's terms, and two to complete the remaining 2 years of Clinton's and Hutchison's terms. Of those 38 seats, the Republicans and the Democrats would be defending 19 each.

Table 6.1 shows the losses made by the president's party in those mid-term elections which fall 2 years into a president's term of office, for such elections occurring since 1914 — the first year of direct elections to both houses of Congress.

Table 6.1 Losses by the president's party in mid-term elections 2 years into a presidential term, 1914–2002

Year	President	Party	Losses by president's party in	
			Senate	House
1914	Woodrow Wilson	D	+5	−59
1922	Warren Harding	Rep	−8	−75
1930	Herbert Hoover	Rep	−8	−49
1934	Franklin Roosevelt	D	+10	+9
1946	Harry Truman	D	−12	−45
1954	Dwight Eisenhower	Rep	−1	−18
1962	John Kennedy	D	+3	−4
1970	Richard Nixon	Rep	+2	−12
1978	Jimmy Carter	D	−5	−15
1982	Ronald Reagan	Rep	+1	−26
1990	George H. W. Bush	Rep	−1	−8
1994	Bill Clinton	D	−8	−52
2002	George W. Bush	Rep	+2	+5

The table shows a considerable variation in fortunes, from the highs — Roosevelt in 1934 and Bush in 2002, who saw their party gain seats in both houses — to the lows, of which Bill Clinton's 1994 debacle is the most recent low point. The table also shows that the Senate is generally much less prone to losses for the president's party than is the House. Indeed, in 6 of the 13 years listed, the president's party actually gained Senate seats in the mid-term elections, and in two other years the president's party lost only one Senate seat. Indeed, the average loss in the Senate for the president's party over this 88-year period is less than two seats. In only two election cycles in the last 60 years — 1978 (Carter) and 1994 (Clinton) — has that average been exceeded.

The current party balance in the Senate is 58 Democrats, 40 Republicans and two independents, both of whom tend to vote with the Democrats, giving the Democrats an effective 20-seat majority. The Republicans would need to make an overall gain of 11 seats to regain control of the Senate. This is way beyond the average, and has not been achieved since 1946. Indeed, as we shall see, the Republicans may consider themselves fortunate to make any overall gains at all.

In the House, the average number of seats lost over the same period is 27, though this has been exceeded only once in the last 60 years — in 1994. Indeed, if one takes only the period from 1962, the average falls to just 16. In the House, the current party balance is 258 Democrats and 177 Republicans. Thus the Republicans would need an overall gain of 41 seats to regain control of the House — another pretty impossible target. It therefore seems likely, at

the time of writing, that the Democrats will remain in control of both houses of Congress following the 2010 mid-term elections.

The Democrat-held seats in the Senate

Of the 19 seats being defended by the Democrats, six seem vulnerable to the Republicans. In **Connecticut**, Chris Dodd has a fight on his hands if he is to be re-elected to his sixth Senate term. Dodd has become unpopular in Connecticut for three reasons: first, the time he spent in Iowa in 2007 trying, unsuccessfully, to win the Iowa Democratic presidential caucuses; second, his close ties to the financial industry, which has become controversial during the recent economic downturn; third, a recent ethics scandal surrounding mortgages for his Connecticut and Washington DC homes. Dodd was also confirmed to have prostate cancer in 2009. His likely Republican opponent is former congressman Rob Simmons, a decorated Vietnam War hero. Simmons served three terms in the House of Representatives — first elected in 2000 and defeated in 2006 by just 83 votes. Of the four potentially vulnerable Senate Democrats, Dodd is the most at risk, but there are three other Democrat senators who could also lose their seats.

In **Nevada**, Senate Majority Leader Harry Reid is struggling to be re-elected to his fifth term. Reid was first elected to the Senate in 1986, but his first three elections — 1986, 1992 and 1998 — were all close-run affairs. Indeed, in 1998 he won only 48% of the vote against then Republican congressman John Ensign, who polled 47%. However, in 2004, against a weak Republican opponent, Reid scored a comfortable victory, winning over 60% of the vote, and he followed this with his election as Democratic Party leader in the Senate. In the same year that Reid won his 60%-plus vote in Nevada, the then Senate Democratic leader, Tom Daschle, was defeated in his re-election bid in South Dakota. When in 2006 the Democrats won control of the Senate, Reid became majority leader, a post he still holds today. In a state that voted for Obama 55–43 in 2008, Reid ought to be a shoo-in to keep his Senate seat. The trouble with being Senate Majority Leader, however, as Tom Daschle discovered, is that you are at the centre of almost every legislative battle in Washington, having to take high profile and often unpopular stands on major issues. As a result, Reid's approval rating back home in Nevada has slumped badly. The one factor that may let him off the hook is the Republicans' inability so far to come up with a strong challenger. This race could turn into a real cliffhanger. It's a race the Republicans would love to win.

Also vulnerable is Arlen Specter of **Pennsylvania**. The Democrats' newest recruit, Specter switched from the Republican Party in spring 2009, and has the backing of President Obama for re-election. However, as he tries to win re-election to a sixth term — his first as a Democrat — Specter is still likely to face opposition from long-standing Democrats in the party's April 2010 primary. Winning the Democratic primary is Specter's first hurdle;

his strongest and best-funded opponent is two-term congressman Joe Sestak. Provided Specter wins the primary, his likely Republican opponent in the general election in November will be former congressman Patrick Toomey. Toomey served three terms in the House of Representatives (1999–2005) but did not seek re-election in 2004, choosing rather to challenge Specter in the Senate Republican primary that year — which Specter won, but by less than 2%, and that only after a last-minute endorsement from President George W. Bush. Thus Specter faces something of a double whammy in 2010. It's another race the Republicans would love to win.

A fourth Democrat senator who may face a struggle for re-election in 2010 is Michael Bennet of **Colorado**. Bennet was appointed to the Senate in 2009 to complete the remaining 2 years of the 6-year term to which Ken Salazar was elected in 2004. Salazar resigned from the Senate to become secretary of the interior in the Obama cabinet in January 2009. While Bennet will benefit both from Colorado's tending towards the Democrats and from incumbency, he is entirely untested as a candidate. His re-election campaign will be his first and like Arlen Specter in Pennsylvania, Bennet will face a challenge from a fellow Democrat in the primary. Andrew Romanoff, a former speaker of the Colorado House of Representatives, was disappointed not to have been appointed to the Senate to fill the Salazar vacancy in 2009. He felt he was much better qualified than the political novice Bennet. Provided Bennet wins the primary, his likely Republican opponent in the general election could end up being the state's former lieutenant governor, Jane Norton. Republicans must retain some hope of unseating the unelected Bennet.

A fifth seat which the Democrats may struggle to keep is currently held by Roland Burris in **Illinois** — though the party's chances improved once Burris announced he would not contest the seat. Burris was appointed in 2009 by the then — and later impeached — state governor Rod Blagojevich, and has always been tainted by association with the former governor. Although the Republicans have lost 9 of the last 10 Senate races in Illinois, they see a window of opportunity opening up for them at a time of turmoil for the state Democrats. Rather than repeating their losing strategy of nominating an ultra-conservative — Alan Keyes — in 2004, Republicans hope to field a moderate, 5-term Congressman Mark Kirk, who currently represents a pro-Obama district north of Chicago.

Yet another appointed Democrat senator who is not contesting his seat is Ted Kaufman of **Delaware**, appointed in 2009 to serve in place of Joe Biden until the special election in 2010. Kaufman has announced that he will not be a candidate in that election. Should Joe Biden's son — Beau Biden — enter the race for the Democrats as expected, he would clearly have widespread name recognition. But with the popular Republican at-large congressman (1993–2010) and former state governor (1985–92) Mike Castle now running,

this could prove to be the best chance the Republicans have of picking up a seat from the Democrats. Castle has, after all, won 11 statewide elections already — two for governor, and nine for his statewide House seat, as Delaware has only one member in the House of Representatives. Many Delaware voters may react with muted enthusiasm to the idea of the Biden family seeing the seat as an inherited right.

A third Senate appointee, Kirsten Gillibrand, who was appointed to fill the **New York** seat occupied by Hillary Clinton until January 2009, may find herself ousted in the Democratic primary by former state attorney general Andrew Cuomo, son of the state's former governor, Mario Cuomo. If Cuomo wins the primary, he is likely to hold the seat against the Republican challenger — even if that turns out to be Rudy Giuliani, who at the time of writing was still contemplating a run for the seat. This is much more of a Republican long-shot — unless, that is, things go pear-shaped for the Democrats in 2010.

Thus, at the time of writing — a year before election day — the Republicans appear to have a realistic shot at two Democrat seats (Connecticut and Delaware) with a chance of gaining up to four more (Nevada, Pennsylvania, Colorado and Illinois) if things really go well for them. The trouble is, the Republicans may well have problems holding on to many of their own seats.

The Republican-held seats in the Senate

One factor which makes things difficult for the Republicans in the Senate races in 2010 is that they (at the time of writing) already have five retirees: two in states which Barack Obama won in 2008 and are therefore highly vulnerable — Ohio and New Hampshire — as well as Missouri (also vulnerable), Kentucky and Kansas. Open seats are often more difficult to defend than those in which the incumbent is seeking re-election.

In **Ohio**, George Voinovich is retiring after two terms. Ohio is nowadays the quintessential bellwether state, having voted for the winner in the presidential race in the last 12 elections — that's all the way back to 1964. Voinovich was a popular two-term governor before entering the Senate in 1998 and, without his name on the ticket, the Republicans will struggle to hold this seat. The Republicans have not fared well in recent statewide elections. Incumbent Republican senator Mike DeWine lost heavily — by 12 percentage points — to Democrat Sherrod Brown in 2006. The Republicans lost the state governorship by a similar margin in the same year. To their advantage in this year's Senate race, though, the Republicans have recruited a top tier candidate in Rob Portman, a former Cincinnati-area congressman as well as one-time budget director to President George W. Bush — though the Bush connection could be more of a drag than an asset. At best, place this race in the toss-up column, one in which the Democrats will fancy a pick-up.

It's much the same situation in **New Hampshire**, yet another bellwether state, where Republican Judd Gregg is not seeking a third term. Gregg was criticised for first accepting a nomination by President Obama to be commerce secretary in the new Obama cabinet and then, within days, withdrawing following a policy disagreement with Obama over the new president's economic stimulus bill. As a result, Gregg announced he would not seek re-election to the Senate in 2010. Republican hopes of holding onto the seat were dashed when former senator John Sununu — who lost his re-election bid to Jeanne Shaheen in 2008 — announced he would not be a candidate. The Democrat candidate is two-term congressman Paul Hodes.

Republican Kit Bond is retiring after four terms representing **Missouri** in the US Senate. Missouri is yet another bellwether state. It voted for the winning presidential candidate in every twentieth-century election bar 1956, voted for Bush in 2000 and 2004, but went narrowly for McCain in 2008. The race to succeed Bond is likely to be between two big names — former House Republican whip Roy Blunt, whose father served as the state's governor, and Missouri's Democrat secretary of state Robin Carnahan. Her father, Mel Carnahan, also served as the state governor and was then elected to the Senate in 2000. However, Governor Carnahan was killed in a plane crash. His wife — Robin Carnahan's mother — was then appointed to fill the vacancy left by her husband's death, but she was defeated in a special election in 2002 by Jim Talent, the current junior senator from Missouri. Expect a close result in this Missouri family feud between the Blunts and the Carnahans.

In **Kentucky**, Senator Jim Bunning is also retiring after two terms. Having won re-election by a razor-thin margin in 2004, many Republicans, both in the state and the in the Senate party leadership, were concerned that if Bunning stood for a third term the seat would be lost to the Democrats. One voice echoing these views was his home state colleague and Senate Minority Leader Mitch McConnell. 'Over the past year, some of the leaders of the Republican Party in the Senate have done everything in their power to dry up my fundraising', complained Bunning. It is highly unusual for the announcement of a senator's retirement to increase his party's chance of holding the seat, but this may well happen in Kentucky. Bunning's replacement as the Republican candidate is likely to be the Kentucky secretary of state Trey Grayson. However, with big-name Democrats lining up for their party's Senate primary, you would have to put this Republican seat on the endangered list.

In **Kansas**, senior senator Sam Brownback is retiring after two terms to run for the state governorship. He had always promised Kansas voters that he would serve only two terms in the Senate, but here, in this Republican heartland state, the Republicans would expect to hold on — especially with Democrat governor Kathleen Sebelius, tapped by President Obama as health and human

services secretary, out of the running. The Democrats have not won a Senate seat in Kansas since 1932, so this should stay with the Republicans.

In **Florida**, one-term senator Mel Martinez retired in August 2009 and was replaced by George LeMieux, appointed by state governor Charlie Crist to serve out the remaining few months of Martinez's term. Florida is another swing state. Since 1964, it has gone for the winning presidential candidate in 11 out of 12 elections, the one exception being its narrow vote in favour of President George H. W. Bush in 1992 rather than the eventual winner, Bill Clinton. With popular state governor Charlie Crist likely to be the Republican candidate, this looks less like an obvious Democratic win.

A potentially vulnerable Republican incumbent is Richard Burr in **North Carolina**. The political climate in the state has changed markedly since Burr first won the seat in 2004. Back then, North Carolina was seen as a reliably Republican state, voting Republican in seven consecutive presidential elections, and in 2004 favouring George W. Bush over John Kerry by 12 percentage points. With Burr winning the Senate seat vacated by Democrat John Edwards, the state now had two Republican senators. In 2008, Obama won the state over McCain and Republican senator Elizabeth Dole lost her seat to little-known state legislator Kay Hagen. However, to increase their chances of unseating Burr in 2010, Democrats will need to come up with a top tier candidate — something they had failed to do a year away from the election.

Another vulnerable Republican incumbent is David Vitter in **Louisiana**. In a strong Republican year in 2004, Vitter managed to win the election with just 51% of the vote. Neither have Vitter's chances been helped by his admission in 2007 to 'a very serious sin' relating to his phone number appearing in the records of a Washington DC escort agency linked to prostitution. The married senator made a public confession and apology, but this will doubtless hurt him among Christian, evangelical voters. Another blow to Vitter's chances of survival came in 2009 with the announcement by conservative Democrat House member Charlie Melancon that he would contest Vitter's seat rather than seek re-election to the House.

With so many potentially competitive Senate races — we have reviewed 15 here — it is difficult to predict the likely final outcome. It is often the case that all the toss-up races fall to the same party. If that were to occur, either party could gain up to five or more seats. However, an equally possible scenario is that the final result ends as a wash, with both parties winning and losing some seats.

The House races

It's all quite different in the House. With so few genuinely competitive House races these days (see Chapter 4), the opportunities for making significant gains in mid-term elections are somewhat limited, barring some significant and widespread feeling of discontent among voters directed at the president's party. This is what occurred in 1994, causing an unusually high number of House seats to change hands. It is also significant that, following the 1992 House elections, 111 of the races were decided by less than 10 percentage points — in other words, were genuinely competitive for 1994. But in 2008, only 61 seats were decided by less than 10 percentage points, meaning there will be significantly fewer genuinely competitive seats in 2010 than there were in 1994.

Exactly a year ahead of the election, the highly respected CQ Politics website (**www.cqpolitics.com**) rated 333 seats as 'safe' and identified a further 59 in which one party was favoured to win, making a total of 392 seats. That left only 43 seats as truly competitive at that stage. Of those, CQ Politics rated 26 as leaning Democrat, 11 as leaning Republican and 6 as toss-ups. You could revisit the website during 2010 and see if there has been any movement in these totals and, if so, in which direction. Of particular interest would be five bellwether districts, all rated as toss-ups a year before the election. These districts, and others like them, will be the key to the 2010 House elections (see Box 6.1).

Box 6.1 Five toss-up Democrat-held Districts in the 2010 mid-term elections

Alabama 2
Bobby Bright (D) won this formerly Republican seat in 2008 by just 0.5% of the popular vote. But at the same time, the District voted for McCain over Obama by 63% to 37%, making Bright a top target for Republicans. Their candidate, Martha Roby, is a councillor in the city of Montgomery and seen as a strong recruit. This is a seat the Republicans need to win if they are to make any headway nationally.

Florida 8
Alan Grayson (D) won this seat from Republican four-term incumbent Ric Keller in 2008 by just over 4% of the popular vote. However, Grayson has stirred up controversy in the House during his first term, famously declaring on the House floor that the Republicans' national healthcare policy was 'don't get sick', and if you do, 'then die quickly'. The Republicans are saying Grayson is too liberal for this middle-of-the-road district but they may fail to field a strong enough candidate to retake the seat.

Idaho 1
Walt Minnick (D) defeated freshman Republican Bill Sali in 2008 by just over 1% of the popular vote. Sali had lost votes with his personally abrasive style, and this solidly Republican district — McCain won it 62–36 — voted for Minnick, a conservative, pro-gun Democrat with a folksy style. The Republican candidate — yet to be chosen — will doubtless try to tie Minnick to the liberal Democratic leadership in Washington. It's another district Republicans need to win back.

Maryland 1

Frank Kratovil (D) won this previously traditional Republican seat in conservative eastern Maryland by a whisker in 2008. The moderate Republican incumbent, nine-term congressman Wayne Gilchrest, was ousted in the primary by the more conservative Andy Harris. However, while McCain was beating Obama in the district by 18 percentage points, Harris just lost to Kratovil by less than 1 percentage point. Harris may be back for a rematch.

Virginia 5

Tom Perriello (D) won this district in 2008 by defeating six-term Republican Virgil Goode by just two-tenths of 1 percentage point. Perriello undoubtedly benefited from Obama's coattails and will have to survive on his own in 2010. He has taken some conservative-pleasing positions during his first term, hoping to win re-election in a district that still went for John McCain over Barack Obama in 2008. Goode has ruled out a rematch but there's quite a list of potentially strong Republican candidates hoping to win back this seat in the mid-terms.

Another factor likely to reduce the number of gains for either party is that most of the early retirements announced on both the Democrat and Republican sides of the House were of members who represent districts that tend to support overwhelmingly one party or another. For example, Republican congressman Nathan Deal of Georgia announced early on that he would not seek another House term but would instead enter the race for the state governorship. Deal's district gave more than 75% of its vote to John McCain in the 2008 presidential race. In Hawaii, Neil Abercrombie is also leaving the House to run for governor. Abercrombie's Hawaii district voted overwhelmingly for Barack Obama in 2008.

Once again, the Republicans are likely to have more retirees than Democrats in the House races. Open seats — those with no incumbent — are often more vulnerable, so the Republicans' hope of recapturing control of the House in these elections seems utterly forlorn, barring some significant meltdown by the Democrats. Possible causes of Democrat collapse? Look out for Obama's healthcare reform either to stall or be unpopular, and for the failure of those critical 'green shoots of recovery' to appear on the economic front in time for the mid-terms. By November 2010, the economy will be 'owned' by the Democrats, as will the war in Afghanistan, which rumbles on into its ninth year. The President — who as a candidate so often proclaimed 'Yes we can!' — may discover that the voters expect results, and fast.

Questions

1 Why might there be an unusually high number of Senate races in 2010?
2 What does Table 6.1 tell us about the loss of Senate and House seats by the president's party 2 years into a president's first term?
3 Why is it highly unlikely that the Republicans will regain control of either the House or the Senate as a result of the 2010 mid-term elections?

4 What factors might lead the Democrats to lose the Senate races in Connecticut and Illinois?

5 Discuss the Democrats' chances of holding onto their Senate seats in Nevada, Pennsylvania, Colorado and Delaware.

6 Why is it significant that five Republican senators are retiring in 2010? How easy or hard will it be for the Republicans to hold onto these seats?

7 Which Republican-held Senate seats are most at risk in 2010?

8 What factors make significant Republican gains in the House unlikely in 2010?

Chapter 7

Filling Senate vacancies: democracy, nepotism or corruption?

Recent controversies

What did Lincoln Chafee of Rhode Island and Lisa Murkowski of Alaska have in common while they served together in the US Senate for 4 years, between 2002 and 2006? True, both were Republicans, but more intriguingly, both were appointed to the Senate to replace their fathers. When Senator John Chafee died suddenly in October 1999, the state governor of Rhode Island, Lincoln Almond, appointed Chafee's son to serve out the remainder of his father's 6-year term. Lincoln Chafee was then elected to his own 6-year term in 2000, but lost his bid for re-election in 2006.

In 2002, Senator Frank Murkowski of Alaska was elected governor of his state and therefore resigned from the Senate, with 2 years still remaining of his fourth term of office. His first responsibility as governor was to fill the Senate seat he had just vacated. As his replacement, he appointed his daughter, Lisa Murkowski. In 2004, Murkowski was elected to her own 6-year term.

When Barack Obama was elected president in 2008, he had to resign from the US Senate. The Constitution does not permit members of Congress simultaneously to hold a position in the executive branch of government. Obama was at the time the junior senator from Illinois. Thus it fell to the Governor of Illinois, Rod Blagojevich, to appoint a replacement. Blagojevich appointed Roland Burris, but within weeks of the appointment, Blagojevich was arrested on charges of having tried to trade Obama's vacant Senate seat for personal and political enrichment. Blagojevich was subsequently impeached by the Illinois state House of Representatives and removed from office by the state Senate. At the time of writing, he faces trial on federal corruption charges.

Filling vacancies when an incumbent senator resigns or dies has become a matter of controversy. The period following the 2008 elections witnessed no fewer than six senators arrive in the chamber solely by the appointment of the respective state governor (see Table 7.1). This brought the number of serving senators who began their Senate careers by appointment rather than election to ten. Critics see this as nepotism and even corruption rather than democracy. What's going on? Should the process be reformed?

Table 7.1 Appointed senators since 1989

Name	State	Party	Date appointed	Served until
Dan Coats	Indiana	Rep	3 January 1989	3 January 1999
Daniel Akaka	Hawaii	D	16 May 1990	Still in office
John Seymour	California	Rep	3 January 1991	*3 November 1992
Harris Wofford	Pennsylvania	D	9 May 1991	3 January 1995
Jocelyn Burdick	North Dakota	D	16 September 1992	†14 December 1992
Harlan Matthews	Tennessee	D	2 January 1993	†1 December 1994
Robert Kreuger	Texas	D	21 January 1993	*5 June 1993
Sheila Frahm	Kansas	Rep	11 June 1996	≠6 November 1996
Lincoln Chafee	Rhode Island	Rep	2 November 1999	4 January 2007
Zell Miller	Georgia	D	24 July 2000	3 January 2005
Jean Carnahan	Missouri	D	3 January 2001	*5 November 2002
Dean Barkley	Minnesota	Ind	4 November 2002	†3 January 2003
Robert Menendez	New Jersey	D	17 January 2006	Still in office
John Barrasso	Wyoming	Rep	22 June 2007	Still in office
Roger Wicker	Mississippi	Rep	31 December 2007	Still in office
Roland Burris	Illinois	D	31 December 2008	Still in office
Edward Kaufman	Delaware	D	15 January 2009	Still in office
Michael Bennet	Colorado	D	21 January 2009	Still in office
Kirsten Gillibrand	New York	D	26 January 2009	Still in office
George LeMieux	Florida	Rep	28 August 2009	Still in office
Paul Kirk	Massachusetts	D	24 September 2009	Still in office

* Defeated for election
† Did not seek election
≠ Defeated for nomination

The 17th Amendment

For the first 126 years of the nation's history, US senators were appointed by the legislatures of their respective states. But all that changed — or was supposed to change — when the 17th Amendment was passed in 1913. From 1914 onwards, senators were to be directly elected, just like members of the House of Representatives. The opening sentence of the 17th Amendment proclaimed:

> The Senate of the United States shall be composed of two Senators from each State, elected by the people thereof...

What does the 17th Amendment have to say about the filling up of Senate vacancies in the new era of an elected Senate? The Amendment's second paragraph states:

> When vacancies happen in the representation of any State in the Senate, the executive authority of such State shall issue writs of election to fill such vacancies: Provided, that the legislature of any State may empower the executive thereof to make temporary appointments until the people fill the vacancies by election as the legislature may direct.

In other words, Senate vacancies will be filled by a special election but may be filled temporarily by an appointee of the state governor as laid down by the state legislature.

In most states, a Senate vacancy is filled by an appointee of the state governor until the next set of congressional elections. If the Senate term to which the appointment was made still has 2 or 4 years to run, a special election will then be held to elect someone to serve out the remaining period. If the Senate term has expired, an election for a full 6-year term will be held.

State-by-state variation

The provisions of the 17th Amendment have resulted in a good deal of variation in state laws regarding the filling of Senate vacancies. In 34 states, the state governor has a free hand to fill up such vacancies by appointment. In these states, the governor is under no obligation to appoint someone of the same party as the previous incumbent. Two states — Oregon and Wisconsin — prohibit the state governor from making any appointment to the Senate. Vacancies can be filled only by a special election. A further two states — Oklahoma and Connecticut — strictly limit the circumstances under which the state governor can make appointments to the Senate.

In four states — Arizona, Hawaii, Utah and Wyoming — the state governor is required to appoint a replacement from the same political party as the prior incumbent. In Hawaii, Utah and Wyoming, the governor must choose between three candidates selected by the prior incumbent's state party. When Republican Senator Craig Thomas of Wyoming died suddenly in June 2007 — just under 2 years into his second term — the state's Democratic governor Dave Freudenthal was given the names of three Republicans from which he could appoint a successor: State Treasurer Cynthia Lummis, former Republican state party chair Tom Sansonetti and orthopaedic surgeon John Barrasso. Freudenthal appointed Barrasso who, in November 2008, won a special election to serve the remaining 4 years of Thomas's term.

In seven states — Colorado, Illinois, Iowa, Maryland, Minnesota, New York and Vermont — measures were introduced during 2009 to either do away with or strictly limit the governor's power to fill Senate vacancies. Three of these states — Colorado, Illinois and New York — saw their state governor making Senate appointments during that year.

In Alaska, nobody quite knows what the law is! Following the controversial Murkowski–Murkowski switch in 2002, Alaska changed its state law to require future Senate vacancies to be filled through special elections. However, because state lawmakers passed legislation, and voters approved a ballot measure that changed the law in different ways, it is unclear whether Alaska's governor is able to make temporary Senate appointments or not.

There are, at the time of writing, six members of the Senate who have been appointed rather than elected: Roland Burris of Illinois, Edward Kaufman of Delaware, Kirsten Gillibrand of New York, Michael Bennet of Colorado, George LeMieux of Florida and Paul Kirk of Massachusetts. Roland Burris's appointment — to replace Barack Obama — has already been mentioned. Three were appointed to fill the vacancies of senators who have joined the Obama administration. Edward Kaufman was appointed to replace Vice-President Joe Biden, while Kirsten Gillibrand and Michael Bennet both replaced senators recruited to the Obama cabinet — respectively Hillary Clinton (Secretary of State) and Ken Salazar (Secretary of the Interior).

The Burris fiasco

Burris's appointment was surrounded by controversy. By mid-December 2008, Illinois state governor Rod Blagojevich was already the subject of an FBI investigation into what had been called a 'pay-to-play' scandal — Blagojevich was asking for financial donations from anyone wishing to be appointed to the vacant Senate seat. Burris had indicated that he would like to be considered for the vacancy but that, if appointed, he would not seek re-election in 2010. In early January, Burris made a sworn statement before the committee of the Illinois state legislative committee considering impeachment charges against the Governor that, prior to his being offered the Senate seat at the end of December, 'there was not any contact between myself or any of my representatives with Governor Blagojevich or any of his representatives leading to my appointment to the United States Senate.'

When the new Congress convened at the beginning of January 2009, however, Senate Majority Leader Harry Reid refused to seat Burris because of the controversy still swirling round the appointment. He was eventually sworn into office on 15 January, but by February, Burris was changing his story as more revelations appeared. He now admitted that Blagojevich had asked him to raise funds for him, and that although he had agreed to do so, he hadn't actually been able to raise any money because the Governor was so unpopular. It soon became clear that raising money for himself was no easier. Having originally said that he wouldn't seek re-election in 2010, Burris was now saying he would run and was starting fundraising for his own Senate bid. However, in mid-April the *Chicago Tribune* reported that Senator Burris had managed to raise just $845. Three months later Burris announced that he would leave the Senate when his current term expired after the 2010 elections.

Another piece of nepotism?

In the 2008 elections Joe Biden ran both for the vice-presidency of the United States and for a seventh term in the Senate representing the state of Delaware. He won both races, but as the Constitution forbids anyone from holding executive and legislative posts concurrently, Biden had to resign from the Senate. On 24 November, Delaware's Democratic governor, Ruth Ann Minner, announced that she would appoint Biden's long-time senior adviser Ted Kaufman to succeed him. Kaufman would serve until a special election was held in 2010 to elect someone to serve out the remaining 4 years of Biden's 6-year term. However, the 70-year-old Kaufman had already let it be known that he would serve only until 2010 — he was not interested in being a candidate in the special election. What everyone suspected was that Kaufman had been given the nomination merely to keep the seat warm, so to speak, until 2010 — when Joe Biden's oldest son, Beau Biden, would run for his father's old seat.

Beau Biden was elected Attorney General of Delaware in 2006. He is also a Captain in the Delaware National Guard and in October 2008 his unit was deployed on active service to Iraq. His tour of duty will have ended by 2010 and Biden is, at the time of writing, expected to run for his father's former seat. Like the Chafees and the Murkowskis, the Bidens like to keep the seat in the family.

Filling Hillary Clinton's seat

Hillary Clinton was first elected to the Senate in 2000 and re-elected in 2006. Thus, when Clinton was appointed by Barack Obama as secretary of state, her second term in the Senate still had 4 years to run. The decision about Clinton's replacement fell to New York's Democratic governor David Paterson. At first, it was widely rumoured that the seat would go to Caroline Kennedy — the daughter of President John F. Kennedy. Her uncle, Robert Kennedy, had been elected to the Senate for New York in 1964 and served until his assassination in 1968. It looked like more family intrigue, but Kennedy decided to withdraw from consideration for 'personal reasons'.

The next most likely appointee was thought to be New York state attorney general Andrew Cuomo, the son of the state's former governor, Mario Cuomo. In the end Governor Paterson decided to nominate Kirsten Gillibrand, who had just been elected to her second term in the House of Representatives. Even Gillibrand's appointment was not entirely without controversy. She had been a member of the moderate Blue Dog Democrat grouping in the House and her voting record had been among the more conservative of her House Democratic colleagues. She had a 100% rating from the National Rifle Association, for example, because of her full-hearted support of gun rights. This brought public criticism from liberal interest groups as well as from her former House colleague from New York, Carolyn McCarthy, a vocal supporter of gun control. Indeed, McCarthy was so cross about the appointment that she threatened to run against Gillibrand in the Democratic Senate Primary in 2010, a threat she later withdrew.

Bennet for Salazar in Colorado

When Barack Obama tapped Colorado's senator Ken Salazar to be secretary of the interior, the state's Democratic governor Bill Ritter needed to appoint a replacement for Salazar in the Senate. His choice was relatively uncontroversial — that of Michael Bennet, who will serve the two remaining years of Salazar's first term. There will then be a regular election in 2010 for a full 6-year term — an election in which Senator Bennet has said he will be a candidate. Bennet's appointment could not really be described as family-related or nepotism. His father has never been a United States senator — though he did serve as an aide to Vice-President Hubert Humphrey in the 1960s, and his grandfather was an economic adviser to FDR.

The point here, however, is that Senator Bennet will contest the 2010 election as the incumbent and that gives him huge advantages, both over any Democratic challenger in the primary, as well as his Republican opponent in the general election.

Other appointed senators

If Bennet is elected to his own full 6-year term in November 2010, he will join five other current US senators who began life as an appointed senator but have gone on to a career as an elected one. We have already mentioned Lisa Murkowski and John Barrasso, but there is also Roger Wicker of Mississippi, Robert Menendez of New Jersey and Daniel Akaka of Hawaii. Akaka was appointed to the Senate in 1990 following the death of Senator Spark Matsunaga and has now been re-elected three times — in 1994, 2000 and 2006.

In August 2009, Republican Mel Martinez announced he was resigning from the Senate, where he had represented Florida since 2004, thus opening the way for yet another replacement appointment — the fourth of the year. However, this placed the Florida governor, Charlie Crist, in an awkward situation. When Martinez announced that he would not seek re-election, Crist had indicated that he would run for the seat. So now Crist had to appoint someone to serve out the remainder of Martinez's term who would not stand in the way of his own Senate ambitions. Crist picked George LeMieux, his former chief of staff. This led to accusations of cronyism. 'Charlie Crist came as close as he could to appointing himself to this position', claimed Eric Schultz, a spokesman for the Democratic Senatorial Campaign Committee. Schultz was insinuating that Crist was using LeMieux to keep the seat safe for him until the 2010 election. This brought a counter-claim from Rob Jesmer, executive director of the National Republican Senatorial Committee:

> The Democrats' desperate criticisms ring hollow, especially considering they stayed mum when Joe Biden had Ted Kaufman appointed to keep 'his' seat warm earlier this year.

Kaufman, if you remember, had been a long-time member of Biden's staff. This was surely a case of 'my cronyism is better than your cronyism'.

Earlier oddities

In the 96 years since the 17th Amendment was passed, there have been no fewer than 184 appointed senators, 21 of them in the past 20 years (see Table 7.1). George Mitchell of Maine, who went on to be Senate majority leader, began his Senate career as an appointed senator. Ted Stevens of Alaska was appointed to the Senate in 1968 and went on to serve for 40 years until his narrow defeat for re-election in 2008.

On a few occasions, a male senator who died in office has been succeeded by his wife. When Mel Carnahan of Missouri died just before his election to the Senate in 2000 — but was still elected — his wife Jean Carnahan was appointed to serve for 2 years, though she lost her bid to be elected to the remaining 4 years of her husband's term in 2002. In 1992, Jocelyn Burdick was appointed to the Senate following the death of her husband Quentin Burdick of North Dakota, and in 1978 Muriel Humphrey was appointed to the Senate following the death of her husband — and former Vice-President — Hubert Humphrey.

There have also been examples where a Senate seat has changed party as a result of a Senate appointment. When Republican senator Paul Coverdell of Georgia died suddenly in July 2000, the Democrat governor of the state Roy Barnes appointed his fellow Democrat and predecessor Zell Miller as governor, to fill the vacancy. Miller served out the remaining 4 years of Coverdell's term but did not seek re-election in 2004. Seats also changed parties by appointment in 2002 in Minnesota (from Democrat to Independent) and in 1991 in Pennsylvania (from Republican to Democrat).

Even odder was what happened following the death of Senate majority leader Robert Taft (Rep–Ohio) back in 1953. Ohio governor Frank Lausche appointed a Democrat to replace Taft — Thomas Burke — and that extra Democrat senator meant the majority changed hands from the Republicans to the Democrats in mid-Congress.

More reform?

Although there has been a good deal of disquiet about governors' powers to fill Senate vacancies, the call for reform is somewhat muted and a little confused. Senator Russell Feingold of Wisconsin introduced a constitutional amendment in the 111th Congress (2009–10) to prohibit gubernatorial appointments and require states to fill Senate vacancies solely by special elections. The proposed amendment reads:

> No person shall be a Senator from a State unless such person has been elected by the people thereof. When vacancies happen in the representation

of any State in the Senate, the executive authority of such State shall issue writs of election to fill such vacancies.

This would bring all states into line with the provisions of Oregon and of Senator Feingold's home state of Wisconsin. But, like most constitutional amendments, it stands very little chance of being passed. Although the Senate Judiciary Committee approved the proposal by 6 votes to 3 on 6 August 2009, Senate Majority Leader Harry Reid says he is 'not in favor of [Congress] dictating to a state what they should do'.

At the same time, Congressman Aaron Shock, a Republican from Illinois, introduced legislation into the House of Representatives that would require states to hold special elections to fill all Senate vacancies and authorise federal funding to reimburse states for up to 50% of the costs of these special elections.

Just as some members of Congress were pushing hard to stop appointments to the Senate, Senator Edward Kennedy was trying to get his state of Massachusetts to return the power of appointment to the governor, which was abolished just 5 years before. Gravely ill with brain cancer, Senator Kennedy was worried that his seat would remain vacant for at least 5 months after his death and, as the state is reliably Democratic, Senate Democrats would be denied a possibly vital vote during that period. The Massachusetts state law, passed in 2004, says that Senate vacancies can be filled only by a special election, which cannot occur until after a minimum of 145 days after the seat falls vacant. In August 2009, Senator Kennedy wrote to the Democrat governor, Deval Patrick, and state legislative leaders:

> I therefore am urging you to work together to amend the [2004 state] law through the normal legislative process to provide for a temporary gubernatorial appointment until the special election occurs.

Massachusetts changed from governor-appointed to directly elected Senate replacements in 2004, when Massachusetts Democrats wanted to stop the then Republican governor, Mitt Romney, from filling a vacancy if Senator John Kerry of Massachusetts defeated George W. Bush in that year's presidential election. As the *Boston Globe* reported, the Massachusetts state legislature passed the new law to remove the governor's power of appointment to Senate vacancies after being 'prodded by a personal appeal from Senator Edward Kennedy'. It would appear that in 2009 Kennedy had undergone a convenient change of mind. One rather waspish writer to the *Wall Street Journal* following the August 2009 story of the Senator's recent letter suggested, tongue in cheek:

> Why don't they just change the law as follows: if a Democrat is governor the seat is appointed; if a Republican is governor a special election is required? There, problem solved!

Following Senator Kennedy's death in September 2009, the Massachusetts state legislature did pass a law restoring the power of the governor to appoint an interim senator until an election was held in January 2010. Governor Deval Patrick appointed Paul Kirk, a former chairman of the Democratic National Committee, to fill the vacancy. Kirk became the fifth senator to be appointed in 2009.

Conclusion

Given the controversy surrounding recent Senate appointments, the number of appointed senators currently holding office and the intentions of the framers of the 17th Amendment, it seems only right that all senators should be elected to office. The argument, put forward most recently by Edward Kennedy, about a state being denied one senator in the intervening period is somewhat specious. States often lack full Senate representation for a period, for a number of reasons. What about the time senators Barack Obama (Illinois), Hillary Clinton (New York), John McCain (Arizona) and others spent on their presidential campaigns in 2007 and 2008? Senators Edward Kennedy (Massachusetts), Robert Byrd (West Virginia) and Tim Johnson (South Dakota) all missed months of debates and votes recently because of serious illness. It was not thought necessary to appoint temporary senators at those times, so why do so when a senator resigns or dies midway through their term of office?

Senate appointments are an anachronism. An appointed senator is given a huge advantage as an incumbent at the next election. Senate appointments have had a nasty habit of turning into acts of nepotism at best, and corruption at worst. Having said all that, nothing much is likely to change in terms of constitutional amendment or federal law. The only change that could take place would be incremental — with each state deciding to change its own state law to require all future senate vacancies to be filled by special election.

Questions
1 How many senators were appointed in the period following the 2008 elections? Give some examples of those who were appointed.
2 How were senators chosen between 1788 and 1914?
3 When and how was this changed?
4 What does the 17th Amendment say about the filling of Senate vacancies?
5 How is this done in most states?
6 Which two states prohibit any Senate appointments by the state governor?
7 What is the procedure for filling Senate vacancies in Wyoming? What happened in Wyoming in 2007?
8 Why can the appointment of Roland Burris to the Senate be seen as 'a fiasco'?
9 What happened when Joe Biden resigned from the Senate to become vice-president?

10 What happened in Florida when Senator Mel Martinez resigned in August 2009?
11 What was extraordinary about the appointment of Zell Miller to the Senate in 2000?
12 What proposals have been introduced in Congress to end appointed senators?
13 What happened in Massachusetts following the death of Senator Edward Kennedy in 2009?

Chapter 8

Change or more of the same?
An assessment of Barack Obama's first year in office

> If there is anyone out there who still doubts that America is a place where all things are possible, who still wonders if the dream of our founders is alive in our time, who still questions the power of our democracy, tonight is your answer.

So spoke President-elect Barack Obama just a few hours after the news media had declared him the winner of the 2008 presidential election. He was addressing a vast and ecstatic crowd in Grant Park, Chicago, just before midnight. Wisely, Obama did not just wow the crowds, he also warned them:

> The road ahead will be long. Our climb will be steep. We may not get there in one year or even in one term but, America, I have never been more hopeful than I am tonight that we will get there. This victory is not the change we seek; it is only the chance for us to make that change.

The crowds roared back — as they had done at rallies across the length and breadth of the country for the past year — with a deafening 'Yes, we can! Yes, we can!' That was 4 November 2008.

As I begin to write this piece, it is 4 November 2009. Of course, Obama has been president for less than a year — his inauguration was not until 20 January 2009. However, as the calendar has swept us along 1 year since that momentous day in November 2008, it is a good opportunity to take the first — if rather cautious — look back over the President's first year in office and ask whether or not he has begun to deliver that much-promised 'change', or whether the Obama presidency looks like 'more of the same'.

How is Obama's public approval rating holding up compared with other presidents at this stage in their administrations? How successful has he been at addressing those most difficult domestic issues that confronted him from Day 1 — the economy and healthcare reform? How effectively is he addressing those major areas of concern in US foreign policy — Iraq, Iran, Afghanistan — as well as delivering on his promise to close the controversial detention facility at Guantánamo Bay? How effectively is he working with Congress? Can we learn anything from the off-year elections held in November 2009? Does the President have an effective governing style? These are the questions we will attempt to address here.

In doing so, however, I am conscious that in the time between my writing this piece and a reader coming to these pages, things are likely to have moved on — maybe quite significantly. So I will from time to time suggest that you, the reader, revisit some of the sources I have used to see if and how things have changed.

Obama's job approval rating

One of the most talked about pieces of evidence when it comes to judging the success, or otherwise, of a presidency is the president's job approval rating. The Gallup polling organisation has been asking the question 'Do you approve or disapprove of the way X is handling his job as president?' every month since the presidency of Harry Truman in 1945. The president's job approval rating is published each month and gives a useful benchmark for judging public opinion on how the president is doing at any particular time.

Figure 8.1 shows President Obama's job approval rating during the first 9 months of his presidency. On 21 January 2009, the first day of the Obama presidency, the President enjoyed a 67% approval rating. It remained above 60% for most of the period until mid-July, but then fell to 50% by late August, before recovering a little in September and October. One year after his election, President Obama's approval rating, as measured by the Gallup polling organisation, was 53%. You can visit the Gallup website at **www.gallup.com** to see how Obama's approval rating has changed since November 2009. Click the 'Obama Job Approval' button on the home page.

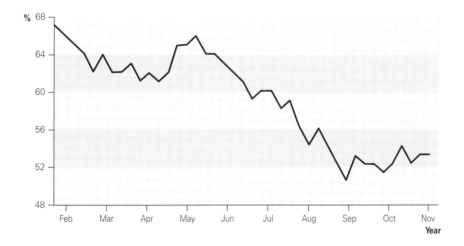

Figure 8.1 Obama's job approval rating, 20 January – 4 November 2009

Source: www.gallup.com

Historically, this is not particularly impressive, as shown in Figure 8.2. Placing Obama alongside his eight elected predecessors, this puts Obama in joint 7th position out of 9. However, it should be pointed out that the president's approval rating 1 year after election gives little clue as to his chances of re-election. George H. W. Bush had a 70% approval rating at this stage but was defeated for re-election 3 years later, while Bill Clinton, with his 48% approval rating a year after election, easily won re-election 3 years later.

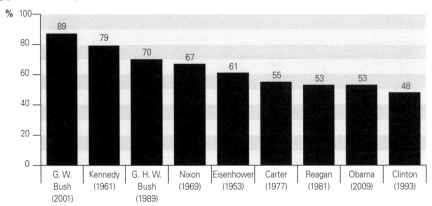

Figure 8.2 Approval ratings 1 year after election: Kennedy–Obama

Source: www.gallup.com

The president's approval rating, however, does affect his ability to get things done — public approval and professional reputation are linked. As Richard Neustadt explained in his classic book on the presidency, *Presidential Power* (John Wiley, 1960), because members of Congress think about the president's public approval rating, 'public standing is a source of influence for him, another factor bearing on their willingness to give him what he wants'. In other words, the more popular a president is, the more he can get done, and the more he gets done the more popular he is likely to be. The downward spiral applies too, and as Figure 8.3 shows, the public's belief in the President has fallen off significantly in the year since his electoral victory. In all eight of the policy issues shown, voters were less optimistic about Barack Obama in October 2009 than they were just 11 months earlier.

The economy

It was clear from the exit poll data at the 2008 elections that Obama benefited hugely from Americans' perceptions that President Bush had mishandled the US economy during his period of stewardship. Between 1 January and 20 November 2008 — much of Bush's last year in the White House — the Dow Jones Industrial Average lost nearly 6,000 points, or 43% of its value. On the day Barack Obama was sworn into office (20 January 2009), the Dow Jones stood at 8,280. On 14 October it closed at 10,005, its first close above 10,000 in over a year. In the first 9 months of the Obama presidency, the Dow

Jones had therefore risen by just over 20%. To see what has happened since, visit **www.mdleasing.com/djia.htm**.

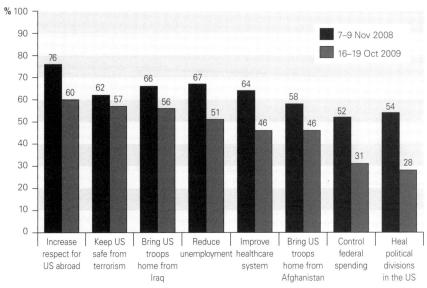

Figure 8.3 Will the Obama administration be able to do each of the following? (% yes it will)

Source: www.gallup.com

Other indicators, though, were less flattering. We commented in Chapter 1 that President Bush saw the unemployment rate increase from 4.2% to 7.2% during his watch. By October 2009, this figure was up to 10.2%. To see what has happened since, visit the Bureau of Labor Statistics' website at **www.bls. gov**. Figure 8.4 shows that the steep rise in unemployment begun in early 2008 has continued throughout 2009.

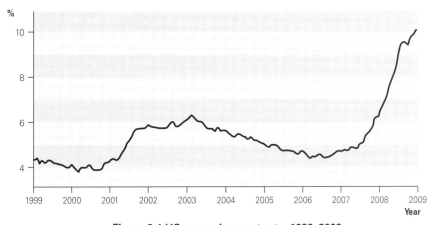

Figure 8.4 US unemployment rate, 1999–2009

Source: Bureau of Labor Statistics

Having signed his $787 billion economic stimulus package into law on 17 February 2009, Obama needs to be able to show results from this huge investment in infrastructure, education and tax breaks sooner rather than later. Otherwise, it won't be long before the ownership of the economic woes of the United States will pass from George W. Bush to Barack Obama, and that could prove a problem for the Democrats in the 2010 mid-term elections. Speaking to the press after a cabinet meeting on 23 November 2009 — the fifth thus far of his administration — President Obama had this to say:

> Our economy is growing for the first time in more than a year. But having said that, we cannot sit back and be satisfied given the extraordinarily high unemployment levels that we've seen. I will not rest until businesses are investing again and businesses are hiring again and people have work again.

Unemployment could become Obama's Hurricane Katrina — the problem that convinces ordinary voters that the President has neither gauged the magnitude of the problem nor has come up with a solution sufficient to address it.

Healthcare reform

Unlike most developed countries, the United States has no universal healthcare system. By 2008, an estimated 46.3 million Americans — or 15% of the population — had no healthcare insurance at all. A further 26% were having difficulties paying their medical bills. There are programmes available that cover certain groups — Medicaid for the poor, Medicare for the 65s and over, and SCHIP (State Children's Health Insurance Program) for children of parents who are fairly poor but not poor enough to qualify for Medicaid.

The costs of healthcare provision are rising, from around $0.25 trillion in 1980 to $2.25 trillion in 2008. The federal government alone spends around $750 billion a year on healthcare — over half of it on Medicare — and with America's population getting progressively older, that figure is set to rise in years to come. Various presidents have tried over the course of more than a century to achieve universal healthcare, but all have failed — most recently Bill Clinton in 1993–94.

Obama made healthcare reform a major part of his 'change' agenda during the 2008 election campaign. His plan called for the creation of a national health insurance exchange, which would include both private- and public-run options. Since he arrived at the White House, however, Obama has left the detail of healthcare reform legislation to Congress — a matter we shall return to later. When the President addressed a joint session of Congress in September 2009, he was still keeping his options open, signalling that he would compromise by stating that 'we should remain open to other ideas that accomplish our ultimate goal'.

Through much of 2009, both houses of Congress worked in committee to put together a healthcare reform bill which would pass their respective chambers. In the House, three committees worked on healthcare legislation — Energy and Commerce, Education and Labor, as well as Oversight and Government Reform. The bill, which eventually came to the floor of the House on 7 November as the Affordable Health Care Act for America, was an amalgamation by the House Democratic leadership of these three committees' bills. On the morning of the debate, the President returned once more to the Capitol, this time to address a meeting of House Democrats whom he urged to 'answer the call of history' and pass the bill. It passed the House by 220 votes to 215. The 220 'yes' votes were cast by 219 Democrats and one Republican; the 215 'no' votes by 176 Republicans and 39 Democrats.

Two weeks later, on 21 November, it was the Senate's opportunity to debate healthcare — or rather, because of the antiquated rules of the Senate, to debate whether to debate healthcare. In the Senate, two committees had drawn up healthcare legislation — the Health, Education, Labor and Pensions Committee and the Finance Committee. These two proposed bills had then been formed into one bill by majority leader Harry Reid. On that November day, the Democrats needed to get 60 votes to break a Republican filibuster of the motion to begin debate on the detail of the bill. After some 10 hours of debate, the Senate voted 60–39 to cut off debate, thereby ending the Republican filibuster and paving the way for the healthcare debate proper to take place at a later time. The vote was entirely along party lines — 58 Democrats and 2 Independents voting 'yes' and 39 Republicans voting 'no'. Republican George Voinovich of Ohio did not vote.

There are many hurdles to be crossed. True, the House has passed a version of healthcare reform but, at the time of writing, the Senate has yet to do even that. There are two Democrats — Ben Nelson of Nebraska and Blanche Lincoln of Arkansas — who have said they will not vote for a bill that includes the so-called public option. Independent senator Joe Lieberman of Connecticut, and possibly some pro-life Democrats, will not support a bill that fails to contain the Stupak-Pitts Amendment which was included in the House version but not, as yet, in the Senate version. The amendment prohibits use of federal funds 'to pay for any abortion or to cover any part of the costs of any health plan that includes coverage of abortion', except in cases of rape, incest or danger to the life of the mother. Once the Senate manages to pass its own healthcare reform bill — if indeed it does — the House and Senate versions would then go to a conference committee, which would need to come up with a compromise version of  the two bills, acceptable to both houses. Healthcare reform still seems a long way off.

Foreign policy issues

> Mark my words, it will not be six months before the world tests Barack
> Obama like they did John Kennedy. Watch, we're going to have an interna-
> tional crisis, a generated crisis, to test the mettle of this guy.

So stated Joe Biden during the 2008 election campaign, in what was one
of his less helpful remarks on the campaign trail. The Obama team at the
time were livid that Biden had made such a comment. It seemed to play into
the hands of Obama's opponents by reminding them of his lack of foreign
policy experience. Hillary Clinton had tried to raise the same issue during the
Democratic primaries with her famous '3 a.m. phone call' television advert:
whether this youthful senator, with limited experience on the world stage,
would be tough enough to handle the high-stakes crises that were bound to
come his way if elected to the presidency.

While the opening months of the Obama presidency brought nothing to rival
Kennedy's Bay of Pigs or Berlin crises of 1961, the newly elected president
did have to deal with such concerns as Afghanistan, Iraq, Iran, the usual
problems of the Middle East, a debut performance at the United Nations
and hosting the G20 economic summit in Pittsburgh. A summary of the
President's performance thus far in terms of foreign policy might be 'no gaffes,
no breakthroughs', as David Broder commented in the *Washington Post* in
late September.

To Broder, a veteran Washington-watcher, the 'no gaffes' bit of this
achievement was largely due to the stellar foreign, defence and national
security team Obama had put together, what Broder called 'Obama's A-Team'.
According to Broder:

> Official Washington is starting to realise that in addition to his personal
> skills, Obama has assembled a highly professional and effective national
> security team that serve him and the nation very well.

His decision to ask Robert Gates to stay on from the Bush administration as
secretary of defense has so far proved to be a good one. He then bolstered
the team by picking retired Marine general James Jones as national security
adviser, according to Broder 'another widely respected veteran of past administrations and a man of great self-discipline and few ego needs'.

The choice of Hillary Clinton to be secretary of state was something of a
puzzle. Why would Obama want her as secretary of state and, even more
puzzling, why would she want to be secretary of state? In this first year, the
decision seems to have worked well. Clinton has demonstrated her usual
passion for hard work, and her less-than-usual ability to act as a team player.
The Gates–Jones–Clinton troika appears to be working as smoothly as the

Dick Cheney–Brent Scowcroft–James Baker partnership of the George H. W. Bush administration, often seen as 'the dream team' for foreign policy. As Broder concluded about the Obama A-Team, 'tougher tests undoubtedly await, but so far the team looks really good'.

In a long-expected speech on 1 December 2009, the President announced both a bold military escalation into Afghanistan in early 2010 and his intention to begin pulling American troops out of the country in July 2011. This 'revolving-door policy' is a clear acknowledgement of the fragile state of public opinion on Afghanistan in the US at large and within the Democratic Party in particular. What it also showed was that Obama is not the gut decision-maker that George W. Bush was. Criticised for 'dithering' by some, Obama makes decisions that are well thought out and are the product of a complex decision-making process, but which are not entirely leak-proof.

Relations with Congress

Unlike his two immediate predecessors, Barack Obama had served in Congress before his election as president, but only for 4 years. Certainly Obama could not boast the kind of congressional experience that Lyndon Johnson (1963–69) brought to the office, having served in Congress for 24 years. This was doubtless one of the reasons why Obama chose Senator Joe Biden as his vice-president — Biden had been in the Senate for 36 years.

To Biden's unparalleled congressional experience he added Rahm Emanuel as White House chief of staff and Phil Schiliro as assistant to the president for legislative affairs — the *de facto* head of congressional liaison. Emanuel has served both in the Clinton administration and in the Democratic leadership team in the House of Representatives and so he knows operations at both ends of Pennsylvania Avenue. Schiliro has served for 25 years as a senior congressional staffer — as chief of staff both to the Democratic congressman Henry Waxman and to the House Committee on Oversight and Government Reform. Indeed, Team Obama is full of former congressional aides, plucked from the senior staff ranks of both houses: Lisa Konwinski, Schiliro's deputy, spent a decade on the staff of Senator Kent Conrad; Melody Barnes, the domestic policy director, used to be the late Senator Ted Kennedy's senior staffer.

The frequent gridlock in Washington is often blamed on the heightened levels of partisanship in Congress, but Obama believes there is another reason: a longstanding mistrust between the White House and Capitol Hill that, as it were, stare at each other down Pennsylvania Avenue like two fighters in an old Western movie.

In a *New York Times* article (7 June 2009) entitled 'Taking the Hill' (i.e. Capitol Hill), Matt Bai claimed that Obama's courtship of Congress has far exceeded

anything tried by his immediate predecessors and that this aggressive courtship is devised and executed by Rahm Emanuel:

> Emanuel has taken an unusually personal role in handling Congress. One of the first things he did as chief of staff was to give out his cell phone number to every Democratic senator (and some Republicans too), and he occasionally pops up on the House floor, talking with one member or another. His social calendar is taken up by dinners with former House colleagues on both sides of the aisle, often at one of the trendy downtown restaurants he favors.

Emanuel claims that the Obama White House has learnt a number of significant lessons from the shortcomings of the Clinton administration. In its relations with Congress, the Clinton White House was 'leadership-driven'. By that, Emanuel means that Clinton's congressional liaison staff tended to deal only with the Democratic leadership in Congress — the Speaker, the majority leaders and a few key committee chairmen. Emanuel believes that to be successful, you need to cultivate relationships with rank-and-file members in both chambers, even both parties. So, according to the White House legislative affairs office, which keeps a track of these things, in just the first 4 months of the Obama presidency, some 320 House members and about 80 senators had visited the White House.

The textbooks tell us that presidents work with Congress not just through people, but through perks. (See, for example, Anthony J. Bennett: *US Government & Politics*, 3rd edition, Philip Allan Updates, 2009, pp. 271–72.) The Obama White House has become uncannily clever at mobilising these 'perks' to their best advantage. When Emanuel is meeting members of Congress in his office — in the opposite corner of the West Wing's ground floor to the Oval Office — he will arrange for the President to do what he calls a 'spontaneous drop-by'. Explains Emanuel:

> I'll be having a lunch here, and the President will just drop by and say hi to [Republican senator] Susan Collins. It's an efficient use of his time.

To what extent this style of congressional courtship of Congress will work is still to be decided. When the American Recovery and Reinvestment Act of 2009 had its final passage votes in Congress in February, only three Republican senators supported it. All the Republicans in the House voted 'no' in what was an entirely party line vote. When the American Clean Energy Act — the so-called 'cap and trade' bill — passed the House in June 2009, only eight Republicans voted 'yes'. Not much evidence of bipartisanship there. The situation was much the same when the Senate voted on the confirmation of Sonia Sotomayor as an associate justice of the Supreme Court: just nine Republicans voted 'yes', with the remaining 31 voting 'no'.

The off-year elections

The year between the presidential election and the mid-terms is referred to as the off-year election. It's a quiet election year compared to those either side of it, with just two state governors' races — those in New Jersey and Virginia. In 2009, 1 year on from Obama's election victory, the Democrats lost both races, which included the defeat of the Democrat incumbent governor of New Jersey, Jon Corzine. Both states had been won by Obama in 2008: Virginia by 5 percentage points (52–47) and New Jersey by a whopping 15 percentage points (57–42). It's dangerous to read too much into these off-year results but, nonetheless, there were three particular signs which might worry the Obama White House: the problem of the economy, the Democrats' share of the vote among independent voters, and the absence of young voters.

The problem of the economy

The dominant issue in the way people voted wasn't healthcare but the economy, and on that issue the Republicans clearly won. In 2008 in Virginia, of the 53% of voters who told exit pollsters they were 'very worried' about the nation's economy, 59% voted Democrat and just 40% Republican. In 2009, of the 54% of voters who said they were 'very worried' about the economy, a mere 23% voted Democrat, with 77% voting Republican — a 37 percentage-point gain by the Republicans. A similar shift occurred in New Jersey, with the Republicans picking up 23 percentage points among this same category of voters.

When Virginia voters were asked which one issue mattered most in deciding how they voted in 2009, 24% said 'healthcare', but 47% said 'the economy and jobs'. The same 2–1 majority for 'the economy' over 'healthcare' was also evident in New Jersey. Remember Bill Clinton's campaign slogan in 1992? 'It's the economy, stupid!' In these two states, it was 1992 all over again, except this time, the Republicans won the economy argument. If the economy does not significantly improve by 2010, the Democrats might expect a mauling — with or without healthcare reform.

The Democrats' share of the vote among independent voters

The Democrats' share of the vote among independent voters has significantly declined since 2008. In Virginia, independent voters made up roughly 30% of the electorate in both 2008 and 2009, but while in 2008 they split their votes between the Democrats and Republicans 49%–48%, in 2009 the split was 33%–66% — a fall of 16 percentage points for the Democrats. The same thing occurred in New Jersey, where the Democrats' share of the independent vote fell from 51% in 2008 to just 30% in 2009. In both states, therefore, independents broke heavily for the Republicans. Nationally, Barack Obama won 52% of the independent vote in 2008, to 44% for John McCain. Obama needs

to reconnect with independent voters, and big government programmes like those he espouses for healthcare and the economy are unlikely to be much of an attraction to them.

The absence of young voters

Another key ingredient of Obama's 2008 victory — young voters — stayed at home in 2009. In Virginia in 2008, voters aged 18–29 made up 21% of the electorate and 60% of them voted for Obama. In Virginia in 2009, 18–29-year-olds made up just 10% of the electorate and only 44% of them voted Democrat. It was the same story in New Jersey, where 18–29-year-olds fell from 17% to 9% of the electorate and their support for the Democrats fell from 67% to 57%.

As Dan Balz reported in the *Washington Post* (4 November 2009):

> Neither [of these two] elections amounted to a referendum on the President, but the changing shape of the electorates in both states and the shifts among key constituencies revealed cracks in the Obama 2008 coalition and demonstrated that, at this point, Republicans have the more energised constituency going into the midterm elections.

Obama's governing style

Barack Obama is the first elected president to arrive in the Oval Office with no direct executive experience since John Kennedy in 1960. Obama's seven immediate elected predecessors had served either as vice-president (Johnson, Nixon and the first George Bush) or as a state governor (Carter, Reagan, Clinton and the second George Bush). We therefore had little to go on regarding his governing or managerial style, except how he ran his presidential campaign which, as we saw in the 2009 *Annual Survey*, was generally regarded as brilliant. Obama's reaction to the economic meltdown in September 2008, as well as his earlier choice of Biden as his running-mate, were likewise praised as being highly competent. What then of his governing style as president?

The first opportunity an incoming president gets to demonstrate his governing and decision-making style is in selecting his cabinet. Here there were some major hiccups — over his initial selections of Tom Daschle as secretary of health and human services and of Bill Richardson and Judd Gregg as secretary of commerce. All three nominations fell by the wayside, prompting the President to a public admission that he had 'screwed up'.

Then there was his executive order on his second full day in office, announcing his intention to close the detention facility at Guantánamo Bay within 1 year. This raised the important question of what to do with the apparently dangerous inmates. George W. Bush had, indeed, kept the facility open mainly because no one in his administration could come up with an answer to this question.

When President Obama was asked about this at the public signing ceremony at the White House, his answer was not exactly convincing:

> And we then provide, uh, the process whereby Guantánamo will be closed, uh, no later than one year from now. We will be, uh… Is there a separate, uh, executive order, Greg, with respect to how we're going to dispose of the detainees? Is that, uh, written?

The President still seemed to be asking questions rather than giving answers. Greg Craig, the person to whom this one was publicly directed, replied: 'We'll set up a process.' Commented Tony Blankley in a piece on the Real Clear Politics website (**www.realclearpolitics.com**):

> To be at the signing ceremony and not know what he was ordering to be done with the terrorist inmates is about equivalent to being a groom at the altar in a wedding ceremony and asking who it is you are marrying.

A criticism that has been made of Obama's governing style during this first year of his presidency is that he has been too hands-off in his dealings with Congress regarding the details of his proposed legislation. This first became a point of comment over the economic stimulus package. Despite having identified the economy as being the make-or-break issue of his first term, Obama was strangely uninvolved in the details of this key piece of legislation. What we saw was his willingness to let the Democratic leadership on Capitol Hill — Nancy Pelosi in the House and Harry Reid in the Senate — design and shape the bill. As the Democratic leadership, especially in the House, is without question tilted towards the liberal wing of the Democratic Party, it was hardly surprising that the legislation saw little support from congressional Republicans.

The same criticism was levelled at the President over his governing style relating to healthcare reform. Obama did not try to dictate to Congress the details of the legislation, leaving that to various congressional committees while merely talking about the general principles he favoured. This was the complete opposite style from that of his Democratic predecessor Bill Clinton. He had the healthcare reform legislation drawn up entirely within the White House — with his wife, First Lady Hillary Rodham Clinton, in charge. In his 1994 State of the Union address to Congress, President Clinton stated clearly:

> If you send me legislation that does not guarantee every American private health insurance that can never be taken away, you will force me to take this pen, veto the legislation, and we'll come right back here and start all over again.

Clinton's was a 'take it or leave it' style, with Congress being presented with what was really a *fait accompli*, but Clinton's healthcare reform failed to reach a vote in either house. Later, writing in his memoir *My Life*, Clinton admitted his tactic of a veto threat had been a mistake.

> I did it because a couple of my advisers had said that people wouldn't think I had the strength of my convictions unless I demonstrated that I wouldn't compromise. It was an unnecessary red flag to my opponents in Congress. Politics is about compromise, and people expect presidents to win, not posture for them.

Obama adopted the opposite style, but he has been criticised by some. 'It's hard to march if you don't have marching orders', commented Charles Jones, political science professor emeritus at the University of Wisconsin and a noted scholar of the presidency. 'If it's "We may go this way or we may go that way", it's hard to go back to the office and say, "We know what we're doing here"', added Professor Jones. Others disagree, such as Democrat senator Sheldon Whitehouse of Rhode Island. He thinks that Obama's hands-off style doesn't show weakness but reflects a strategic decision by the White House about the best way to get major legislation passed.

'Let's have more of LBJ'

Some of President Obama's critics from within his own party want him to be more like LBJ — Lyndon Baines Johnson, president from 1963 to 1969. Speaking to the *National Journal* on condition of anonymity ('Is Obama Tough Enough?', 17 October 2009), one long-serving aide to a Democratic senator remarked:

> He's been all carrots and no stick so far. He has to be more Lyndon Johnson. Half, 'I love you, but I'll stick this screwdriver right through your heart in a second if it is to my advantage.' On the fear question, I don't think he or his team is feared.

Douglas Brinkley, a history professor at Rice University and author of many acclaimed presidential biographies, agrees:

> Nobody is really worried about the revenge of Barack Obama, because he is not a vengeful man. That's what we love about him — he's so high-minded, and a conciliatory guy, and he tries to govern with a sense of consensus — all noble goals, but they don't get you very far in this Washington knifing environment. He needs to be more like LBJ. He has to change his tactical framework, if his personality will allow it, to being a much more in-your-face, cutthroat, high-minded nationalist, pushing the country's agenda to the people.

There is a feeling in Washington that Obama is not tough enough, not confrontational enough, not feared enough. Such conclusions are supported by some of the public setbacks that Obama has suffered during his first year:

- by the Scottish government on the release of the convicted Lockerbie bomber
- by New York governor David Paterson on his re-election bid in 2010
- by former Virginia governor Douglas Wilder on his lack of support for Democrat gubernatorial candidate Creigh Deeds in the 2009 off-year elections
- by the Olympic committee on Chicago's bid for the 2016 games

On each issue, Obama was rebuffed: the Scottish government released the bomber; Governor Paterson says he will still run for re-election in 2010; Wilder announced he would not support Deeds in 2009; and Chicago's Olympic bid fell at the first fence.

Admittedly, all these reversals were played out away from Washington, but in the House of Representatives, 88 Democrats joined the Republicans in a non-binding resolution to forbid the relocation of Guantánamo detainees on US soil. Bruce Buchanan, a professor of government at the University of Texas (Austin), comments:

> There are moments when fear is useful, when people have to realise who's in charge and there may be consequences for bucking the person in charge.

Two counter-arguments need to be kept in mind, however. First, one of the main reasons why Obama has run into difficulties is that he's trying to achieve some big things, and to do them at a time of economic hardship. Clinton had a rosier economy and still failed to achieve big things. According to David Rohde, a political scientist at Duke University:

> He's trying to make big changes. If he were to have proposed a health bill that made just a little, incremental change, it would have flown through the House and Senate with no trouble at all.

Second, comparisons with LBJ are misleading. Johnson did what he did in 1964 and 1965 against the background of the national support he gained following the assassination of John F. Kennedy. In the 1964 election, he won over 61% of the vote and 44 states. In Congress, the Democrats controlled 68 seats in the Senate and had a 295–140 advantage in the House. If Obama's Democrats today had 68 seats in the Senate instead of 60, and 295 seats in the House instead of 258, healthcare reform would barely have been debated — it would just have been enacted. Congress is a much more difficult place for any president to control today than it was in LBJ's day, so the Johnson analogy is of dubious relevance.

Conclusions

During this first year of his presidency, Barack Obama has been criticised both for acting too quickly (wanting healthcare reform by August 2009) and too slowly (Afghanistan). Maybe this contradiction points up a paradox about the President: that he is both progressive and deliberative. Certainly we shall not be using that much-used adjective attached to his predecessor — incurious. This is not a man who goes with his gut reaction without stopping to think and asking the hard questions. A top White House adviser was quoted recently as saying of Obama: 'He wants to hear all sides of an argument thoroughly. And then he makes a decision.'

Obama took office in January 2009 facing an unusual combination of inherited challenges: the economy, Afghanistan, healthcare. All three, one could say, were the product of decades of inaction by presidents of both parties. But as 2009 fades into 2010, we are probably reaching something of a tipping point in the Obama presidency, when the average American, as well as the Washington insider, will be making a decision about Obama's success as president. To conservative Republicans, his actions on the economy as well as his favouring of a public option on healthcare reform have been enough for them to label him a big-government, big-spending liberal. If 'the era of big government [was] over' under Bill Clinton, it's alive and well under Barack Obama, according to them. In contrast, to many liberal Democrats, he's someone who is far too willing to compromise rather than fight for liberal causes. Their evidence would be his unwillingness to pull American troops out of Afghanistan, not appointing an obviously dyed-in-the-wool liberal judge to fill his — thus far — one Supreme Court vacancy, and his willingness to accept too many significant compromises on healthcare reform.

Speaking to an invited audience in London in November 2009, Democrat congressman Sandy Levin of Michigan cautioned against making too quick a judgement on the President, and he was right. What we can say is this: if Obama gets not only his $787 billion stimulus package, but some significant healthcare reform, reform of the financial services industry and progress on climate change, it will be a hugely important achievement, not only for the policy achievements themselves, but it will vindicate Obama's style of governing — that you don't have to knock people around to get things done in Washington.

If, on top of that, Obama can see a real turnaround in the economy — not only in terms of national headline figures, but also how individual Americans feel about their own economic situation — then by the beginning of 2011, he will be in a strong position for re-election. But if not — if healthcare reform falters, climate change goes largely unaddressed, and the economy continues to look grim — then Republican tails, possibly encouraged by some good results in the mid-terms, will be wagging once more and the President's re-election will be far from assured.

Questions

1 What did Barack Obama warn his supporters of in his election night speech in 2008?
2 What does Figure 8.1 tell us about Obama's approval rating during 2009?
3 What conclusions do you draw from Figure 8.2 and Figure 8.3?
4 What happened to the Dow Jones Industrial Average during 2009?
5 What happened to unemployment rates in the US during 2009?
6 How could unemployment become Obama's Hurricane Katrina?
7 What happened on healthcare reform during 2009 in (a) the House of Representatives and (b) the Senate?
8 What international challenges did Obama face during 2009?
9 How did David Broder rate Obama's foreign, defence and national security team?
10 How has Vice-President Joe Biden been able to help Obama in his relations with Congress?
11 How does White House Chief of Staff Rahm Emanuel try to create good relations with members of Congress?
12 What three factors of concern for President Obama were shown in the off-year election results in 2009?
13 What criticisms have been made of Obama's governing style?
14 How did Obama try to avoid the mistakes of President Clinton over healthcare reform?
15 In what ways do some Democrats want Obama to be more like LBJ? Why might this comparison be misleading?
16 What issues are likely to prove decisive in the run-up both to the 2010 mid-terms and Obama's re-election in 2012?

Who's who in US politics 2010

Executive branch

President	Barack Obama
Vice-President	Joe Biden

The cabinet

Secretary of State	Hillary Clinton
Secretary of Defense	Robert Gates
Secretary of the Treasury	Timothy Geithner
Secretary of Agriculture	Tom Vilsack
Secretary of the Interior	Ken Salazar
Attorney General (Justice Department)	Eric Holder
Secretary of Commerce	Gary Locke
Secretary of Labor	Hilda Solis
Secretary of Health and Human Services	Kathleen Sebelius
Secretary of Education	Arne Duncan
Secretary of Housing and Urban Development	Shaun Donovan
Secretary of Transportation	Ray LaHood
Secretary of Energy	Steven Chu
Secretary of Veterans' Affairs	Eric Shinseki
Secretary of Homeland Security	Janet Napolitano

Executive Office of the President personnel

White House Chief of Staff	Rahm Emanuel
Director of Office of Management and Budget	Peter Orszag
Director of National Economic Council	Larry Summers
Chairman of Council of Economic Advisers	Christina Romer
Domestic Policy Council Director	Melody Barnes
National Security Adviser	James Jones
Assistant to the President for Legislative Affairs	Philip Schiliro
Trade Representative	Ron Kirk
Press Secretary	Robert Gibbs

Other executive branch personnel

Director of Central Intelligence Agency (CIA)	Leon Panetta
Director of Federal Bureau of Investigation (FBI)	Robert Mueller
Chairman of the Joint Chiefs of Staff (JCS)	Admiral Michael Mullen

Legislative branch

President *Pro Tempore* of the Senate	Robert Byrd (D–West Virginia)
Senate Majority Leader	Harry Reid (D–Nevada)
Senate Minority Leader	Mitch McConnell (R–Kentucky)
Senate Majority Whip	Dick Durbin (D–Illinois)
Senate Minority Whip	Lamar Alexander (R–Tennessee)
Speaker of the House of Representatives	Nancy Pelosi (D–California)
House Majority Leader	Steny Hoyer (D–Maryland)
House Minority Leader	John Boehner (R–Ohio)
House Majority Whip	James Clyburn (D–South Carolina)
House Minority Whip	Eric Cantor (R–Virginia)

Senate Standing Committee chairs

Agriculture, Nutrition and Forestry	Blanche Lincoln	Arkansas
Appropriations	Daniel Inouye	Hawaii
Armed Services	Carl Levin	Michigan
Banking, Housing and Urban Affairs	Christopher Dodd	Connecticut
Budget	Kent Conrad	North Dakota
Commerce, Science and Transportation	Jay Rockefeller	West Virginia
Energy and Natural Resources	Jeff Bingaman	New Mexico
Environment and Public Works	Barbara Boxer	California
Finance	Max Baucus	Montana
Foreign Relations	John Kerry	Massachusetts
Health, Education, Labor and Pensions	Tom Harkin	Iowa
Homeland Security and Governmental Affairs	Joseph Lieberman	Connecticut
Judiciary	Patrick Leahy	Vermont
Rules and Administration	Charles Schumer	New York
Small Business and Entrepreneurship	Mary Landrieu	Louisiana
Veterans' Affairs	Daniel Akaka	Hawaii

House Standing Committee chairs

Agriculture	Collin Peterson	Minnesota
Appropriations	David Obey	Wisconsin
Armed Services	Ike Skelton	Missouri
Budget	John Spratt	South Carolina

Education and Labor	George Miller	California
Energy and Commerce	Henry Waxman	California
Financial Services	Barney Frank	Massachusetts
Foreign Affairs	Howard Berman	California
Homeland Security	Bennie Thompson	Mississippi
Judiciary	John Conyers	Michigan
Natural Resources	Nick Rahall	West Virginia
Oversight and Government Reform	Edolphus Towns	New York
Rules	Louise Slaughter	New York
Science and Technology	Bart Gordon	Tennessee
Small Business	Nydia Velázquez	New York
Transportation and Infrastructure	James Oberstar	Minnesota
Veterans' Affairs	Bob Filner	California
Ways and Means	Charles Rangell	New York

Judicial branch

		President who appointed	Year
Chief Justice	John Roberts	George W. Bush	2005
Associate Justices	John Paul Stevens	Gerald Ford	1975
	Antonin Scalia	Ronald Reagan	1986
	Anthony Kennedy	Ronald Reagan	1988
	Clarence Thomas	George H. W. Bush	1991
	Ruth Bader Ginsburg	Bill Clinton	1993
	Stephen Breyer	Bill Clinton	1994
	Samuel Alito	George W. Bush	2006
	Sonia Sotomayor	Barack Obama	2009